—— THIS WAS MY ——
WIMBLEDON

THIS WAS MY
WIMBLEDON

A Life of Challenge and Reward for the Ordinary Tennis Player

HOWARD H. NIXON

Best Wishes

Howard Nixon

10.8.2012

authorHOUSE®

AuthorHouse™
1663 Liberty Drive
Bloomington, IN 47403
www.authorhouse.com
Phone: 1-800-839-8640

Published by AuthorHouse   06/01/2012

ISBN: 978-1-4685-0343-2 (sc)
ISBN: 978-1-4685-0344-9 (e)

CONTENTS

FOREWORD

By Jo Cunliffe

WHEN HOWARD TOLD me he was writing a book about tennis I was thrilled and excited. First, that my friend was writing a book and how privileged I was to be keeping it a secret. I was confident that it would reveal his deep love of the game.

There are experiences that have happened in my life, which have shaped my future. Meeting Howard in 2003 was one of them. We met at Tennis World, which is an indoor centre in Middlesbrough. Our shared passion for tennis echoed a similar theme and we have been great friends ever since. The fact there are over 40 years difference in our ages makes it even sweeter that we should have formed such a deep and long lasting friendship because of the game we have both played and enjoyed throughout our lives. Our tales are almost identical with friendships and treasured memories accrued along our tennis journeys.

What is intriguing about Howard's life is the absence of the indoor centres, professional coaches and high technology racquets, something that our budding stars of today sometimes take for granted. Personally I have always believed that it isn't about the best facilities or equipment that creates tennis players . . . it is the hunger, drive and passion that makes you the best you can be. This book confirms some of my thoughts developed over my 27 year tennis history.

Tennis is a game for life. What other sport can you start at 3 and still be playing ninety years later? Howard's unbelievable recollections of certain match points, rivalries and key moments make my hairs stand up in admiration and respect! I am yet to find another fellow tennis player whose passion for the sport is so deep they live and breathe the game as much as Howard.

When Howard told me about the onset of Parkinson's I was devastated and worried that hitting tennis balls would have to be resigned to the locker room. However Howard did not give up, quite the opposite . . . . he found ways to continue playing and adapting his game, truly embracing the grit and determination to not let his commitment wane.

As we all know Wimbledon is a dream that most tennis players can only think about. But what this book so beautifully narrates is that the Wimbledon dream can be emulated within your Club, County or even on holiday. Howard's love of tennis sees him playing overseas whilst on holiday and despite language difficulties seeking out fellow enthusiasts to play and share his joy of a new and different challenge.

All of these wonderful tales and experiences are described with such emotional clarity that I am sure whoever reads these recollection and inspiring stories of a life influenced by the lure of the game will thoroughly enjoy it from start to finish.

INTRODUCTION

T ENNIS HAS BEEN a means of expressing my competitive
instinct and to be challenged by it. Why has it had such
a hypnotic hold on me? Well, what other sport can provide
a gladiatorial combat between players of the same age, or
different ages or even a different sex. What other sport has a
tournament structure that provides competitive play beyond
the age of 80. For those wishing for a more relaxed and light
hearted endeavour club nights and other social club events
provide opportunities for playing consistently throughout
the year and encouraging the expression of their competitive
instinct and creating opportunities of real comradeship
within the social structure of the club.

Throughout my time it has been exciting seeing the
development of the game. The increased opportunities to
play, the use of indoor centres, the ratings system and the
tournament structure are an avenue for further involvement.
The proliferation of coaches at indoor centres and clubs are
an essential ingredient in encouraging the standard of play in
the better players and helping the beginners, often in middle

age, to acquire the skills sufficient for them to enjoy the thrill of competition and beyond.

The essence of competition is to gain an advantage over your opponent but what is so intriguing are the many factors determining the outcome. Good reactions and speed around the court coupled with good racket control may be insufficient if not accompanied by analysing their weakness and exploiting your tactical awareness. You need to be in control of your emotions, as in other aspects of your life, and to accept defeat with good grace and success with modesty.

It is this cauldron of interaction which challenges the core of your very being and provides such character building moments. It brings players closer together and provides a basis for new and lasting friendships.

CHAPTER ONE

THIS WAS MY WIMBLEDON

Participation in Veteran Events, The joy of attainment to play within the romantic environs of the All England Club.

❦ ❦ ❦

T HERE ARE VERY few opportunities to play on the courts at Wimbledon. There are the unique championships which are held each year in June and which are regarded as the most prestigious of all the Grand Slam events, there are occasional Davis Cup matches and tournaments for those in the services. Junior Wimbledon is held there and also the National Veteran Championships of Great Britain.

Initially I did not apply to play at Junior Wimbledon because I felt there was little chance of acceptance. However, when I won my County under 18 Singles title late in August I decided to apply. I was asked to complete an entry form and send it in.

Although it would be classed as a late entry along with 18 others my impression was that I would be allowed to play. There was much controversy at the time about a late entry from Roger Taylor, the most gifted of the British Juniors. He wrongly assumed that the L.T.A. would deal with his acceptance whereas the LT.A. felt he had been negligent in his duty to take responsibility for his own entry. The L.T.A. accordingly along with all other late entries refused to accept his and other late entries. I was devastated and never believed there would again be an opportunity, late in life, to play there if my entry was accepted to play in the British Veteran Championships of Great Britain.

At 46 years of age I decided to apply for entry into the over 45 singles event. I knew little about the standard and entry requirements, but completed the application form and waited for the response. The card arrived! I was to be the 12th match on court 5 at the All England Lawn Tennis Club.

This was to be a special day and one to be treasured. As I drove through the main gates an official saluted me and I soon realised how very professional everything was. I was assigned to the No.1 changing room and as I looked around I began to think about all the great players who, at some time, may have changed there.

I noticed that it had started to rain and in a childish way I began to think that it would rain all day and I would never get to play at Wimbledon. Suddenly the clouds cleared, the sun shone brightly and my opponent T.A. Adamson and I were summoned to the Referee's Room, given the balls and card and told to begin our game on court 5.

I have never enjoyed a knock up so much. It was clear that the weather had changed and would not curtail our game. I was aware of how good my opponent was and although I would try my hardest I was realistic to know that it was unlikely that I would win. I certainly wasn't going to find myself in a stressful situation of big points in particular games which would decide the outcome of the match. I felt capable of winning a few games and able to provide an opposition to my opponent which would make the game enjoyable for both of us. I cannot recall the exact score by which I lost but I do remember getting a couple of games in each set and I think I lost 6-2, 6-3.

The game itself was only part of what made the day special. It was the awareness that within the environs of the All England club there was the opportunity to immerse yourself in the history of the game and to understand its iconic status.

The Wimbledon Museum has an immense amount of material and film to guide you through the history of the game and for you to appreciate all those factors which have and continue to maintain its unique status. Foremost amongst these are the players themselves, who in titanic clashes, have demonstrated skills of the highest order. As in differing levels of performance they reflect the thrill of competition, the execution of skill and the delicate balance between success and failure.

I began to remember about those players I had seen on television or read about in the paper who had played here and committed themselves to the challenge of the Wimbledon crown. Wimbledon evokes memories of some of those unforgettable matches. Borg's loss of that incredible third set and yet he went on to beat McEnroe; Arthur Ashe's tactical restraint of Connor's power; Nadal's consistent retrieving, athleticism and incredible attacking shots, when all seemed lost against Federer are recent examples of not only the quality of play but how these players have responded to the threat of defeat. As a young boy I marveled at the skill of the great Australian players, Laver, Rosewall and Newcome and the sublime entertainment provided by others such as Nastase; the touch play of Santana, the controlled power of the charismatic Hoad and the all-round domination of Sampras.

On the women's side I can still picture the unrestrained joy of Virginia Wade's victory in Coronation Year, the powerful superiority of Navratilova's domination of others, the majestic stroke play of Maria Bueno and the all round talent and feminism of Steffi Graf and Chris Evert and the unrivalled superiority of the Williams sisters. All had graced these courts.

My match was played on the red shale courts because of the amount of rain that day; they lie just beyond the championship courts and I was able to walk around and imagine the earnestness of the players as they contested each point. I looked at the Centre Court and had a fleeting image of myself running on to the court and serving a ball across the court, although there was no net up and a security camera to deter such histrionics. I looked at the fine statue of Fred Perry and marveled at his achievements. No visit to Wimbledon is surely complete without contemplating Kipling's powerful message which adorns the players' entrance: "If you can meet with triumph and disaster and treat those two imposters just the same."

The title "This was my Wimbledon" is intended to show the understandable differences of performance at differing levels of ability and the subsequent goals that we set, but that the emotions we experience are those of shared values. Whether you succeed in reaching the attainment level which permits you to play in the championship proper or struggle to qualify for the veteran events the competitive instinct to succeed and its intended consequences are examples of challenges to be faced by all. The text provides many descriptive examples of how the writer responded to his thoughts, feelings and reaction to critical situations during match play and the lessons which have been learnt. Whatever the level of achievement tennis provides fundamental sporting experiences to be treasured.

Chapter Two

BEGINNINGS

Varied sports practices and development of hand-eye coordination.
The awakening of the competitive spirit.

❧ ❧ ❧

F ROM AN EARLY age I seemed to have an unquenchable
desire for activity and an involvement in pursuing a
competitive challenge. This was partly explained by where
we lived. Our house backed on to the Carlisle Rugby
Ground and in the holidays and other free time it became
our "Theatre of Dreams."

Chris, who was a couple of years younger than me, had
an elder brother who played for the first team and so there
was never a problem about playing there. Throughout the
long school holidays and other free time there was always
an occasion to exploit our opportunities. Sometimes older
children from close by would come and join in and Chris
and I were always put in goal in football matches as we

were the youngest two. We hated this and longed to be more involved in the general play. Cricket was a particular favourite and my father even brought his lawn mower to cut a strip for us! When it was time for lunch my mother would open the kitchen window and ring a bell and the rule was that all activity would cease immediately until the afternoon session!

However, it was on those many occasions, when only Chris and I were around that our earnest competitive challenges began. At the side of the ground there was a line of trees and the distance between two of these trees was an ideal pace for the goal posts. We would take penalties against each other and often play as many as ten games at a time. At the side of the field was a hockey pitch which belonged to a private school and we would climb over the fence and bully off in the centre of the pitch and the first to six or ten goals would win. In a 1 to 1 situation it was more than a little tiring! I can't recall where we got the hockey sticks from but somehow we managed it.

Chris was always able to get a rugby ball and we spent many hours attempting to kick the ball between the posts from different angles, distances and with either foot. I remember on one occasion practising by myself to kick the ball over the posts from the 25 yard line. It was becoming dark and I could not see clearly whether I succeeded and so I began to run after my kick to get a better sighting of the ball. Suddenly I was aware that a figure was moving towards me and so I picked up the ball and ran home as fast as my legs would carry me!

There were also many individual tasks where we would compete against our own score. Head Tennis was one of these where you would attempt to keep the ball up as long as possible. It was comparatively easy with a normal sized leather ball but much more difficult with a tennis ball. I seem to remember my score being 21, which on reflection, was very good. On one occasion we managed to get some golf clubs. Chris was practising his swing without the ball when I, unfortunately, was standing directly behind him. His club hit me directly in the eye so sport was cancelled for the rest of the day while I had to go to the hospital.

The back door to our house at the bottom of the garden was directly in line with a door of similar size which gained entry to the rugby ground. The game started where one of us would throw the ball about a foot higher than the player who would attempt to head it into the opposite goal. After such an attempt the response throw would pass to the other player. The receiver always had the option to complain about the throw if he felt at a disadvantage. We would play up to 10 and such games could last a long time.

There were the usual races over 100 yards and longer distances when we needed a further challenge. There was no doubt that we were both extremely fit.

One of the joys of sport is seeing your friends achieve success and Chris's elevation to international rugby at the age of 28 from the lower echelons of Carlisle's position in the rugby world, classified him as a Cumbrian hero on a par with Chris Boddington, the Everest leader, Bill Teasdale, the fell runner whom no one in the world could beat and Eddie

Stobart, who built up an international haulage company respected throughout the world.

Chris so dominated Cumberland and Westmorland rugby matches against higher opposition that his talent could no longer be ignored and he was chosen for the Barbarian Easter Tour in Wales in the Easter of 1971. I remember particularly a Telegraph writer saying that "Philip Sella, the French three quarter, was one of the finest players in world rugby but he was completely overshadowed by Chris Wardlow on this tour." It was to be hoped that he would not drop out of the public eye. He broke up the successful Duckham and Spenser partnership, which allowed the selectors to include him in the team. In that season's match against Ireland, which England won 9-3, all the broadsheets confirmed that he was the outstanding player on the field. He was selected for the successful 1971 Lions team in New Zealand but was unable to go because he fractured his jaw shortly before the Tour began.

He was a wonderful utility player and gained his first cap at full back as a replacement for the English captain, Bob Hiller, who was injured when playing against South Africa. He played for the Barbarians as a fly half and winger and in the matches for England, as a centre three quarter. He was instrumental in helping the Northwestern Counties become the first regional team to beat the All Blacks in Britain. A text: the "All Blacks in the Lion's Den" quotes the coach John Burgess saying, "Wardlow was the key man in our tackling around the scrum which restricted their attacking ploys . . . and his tackling was one of the great features of the game."

I like to think that the many varied games that we played in our teenage years contributed to the athleticism, ball handling skills and, tactical awareness displayed so admirably on the international scene.

It was my intense interest in reading about his exploits that got me, on one occasion, into serious trouble with my father in law. He had a popular cafe in the tourist town of Conwy in North Wales and in the long summer holidays I had, as a teacher, worked in the cafe behind the scenes. At the back of the cafe and down two steps there were two machines which I operated and from which I could provide the chips ready to be fried in the kitchen of the cafe. The first stage was to pour the potatoes from a bucket into the first machine which peeled them and then after they had been checked and considered ready for cutting, to take them out of the first machine and pour them into the second machine which would then slice them up into the appropriate shape.

This was the day after the Easter tournament had begun and the Barbarians had played their first match in which Wardlow had played outstandingly well. I was reading the Telegraph and became oblivious to my key responsibility when my father in law appeared in quite a distressed state because they had run out of chips and the cafe was completely full. He hastily picked up a bucket, held it to the door of the machine and released the peeled potatoes into the bucket. They were the size of marbles! He was more than a little unhappy!

My very earliest experience of developing and acquiring ball skills was with my father, who played cricket for Carlisle, and who spent many an hour teaching me the basic skills of batting. He had part of the garden cemented so that we could practice in all weathers. He would throw balls at me of varied flight and taught me exactly how to play them. He was adamant that it was always necessary to move my feet. I had extra coaching in the nets at the Carlisle cricket ground and so naturally had a dominance in cricket skills in relation to other pupils of the same age.

I remember playing for my school preparatory team against another private school and I hit the ball so consistently to the boundary that rather than be excited I became increasingly frustrated because it was taking so long to retrieve the ball from the long grass. I felt supremely confident in my batting not because of any belief in outstanding natural ability but because of the coaching which had prepared me so well.

At an early age in the Senior School I was chosen for the school team and my name was posted on the wall to play in a match on the Saturday. I turned up barely able to contain my excitement when the captain told me there had been a change of plan and I was no longer needed. I was devastated and it was clearly the blackest day of my school life. I felt I never wanted to play cricket again and it was then that I turned my attention to tennis. I was about 13 to 14 years of age.

On a lighter note I recall the many times we went on holiday and my father and I would find the nearest park so I could practice my fielding skills. I would stand about 30 metres away and my father would use a tennis racket to hit the ball long and high into the air. Often I could only catch it by running as fast as I could either forwards, backwards or even to the side before diving to catch the ball as it was close to landing on the ground.

I remember an occasion when playing cricket and an old man was asleep in his deck chair which was positioned at the top of his garden. The garden sloped down towards the road and so it was clear to see him there. My father bowled to me and I struck the ball early which sent the ball an enormous distance and high into the sky. The ball landed either on him or close to him and he jumped up as if he had been shot! I had never seen my father laugh so much as he did on that day.

A key factor in the earliest development of my balls skills was influenced by what I had read in the autobiography of Don Bradman, the greatest Australian cricketer. He was convinced that his hand-eye coordination developed as a result of him throwing a golf ball against a wall and catching it. Needless to say I followed this routine most days and found that if you angled the ball towards the ground before it struck the wall the extent of variability in the return was very unpredictable. You could also increase the complexity of the skill by varying the speed of the throw.

CHAPTER THREE

SCHOOLDAYS AND COMPETITIVE SPORT

Early experiences of tournament play. School, City and County
Singles champion, analysis of success and other responses.

◦ ◦ ◦

I FAILED THE 11+ exam necessary for a grammar school
education and so my parents decided that my best
opportunity to achieve the 5 subjects at O-level, necessary
for college entrance, lay in a change of school. Austin Friars
School was an independent catholic school but did admit
non-catholics on a fee paying basis.

I was admitted to the school but had to spend a year in
the preparatory school before entering the senior school. My
first day at the new school was quite bizarre and certainly not
representative of a normal school day. I was sat at my desk
about 15minutes after the start of the lesson and had still not

been given any exercise books or writing materials. My desk was bare.

The headmaster came into the room and spent a few minutes talking to the teacher and then left. The class teacher then said that when the headmaster comes into the class we should get out one of our textbooks and read it.

He complained that we hadn't done this and so he went round the class and using the edge of a wooden ruler caned us all! I was too nervous to point out that I had no books to read and so I took my punishment. I told no one until this day! How different from the day I left. I was tearful knowing that this was my last day in school. I loved the schools emphasis on high academic standards, its emphasis on the value of sport and opera and its insistence on acceptable behaviour. The majority of lessons were taught by the Augustinian priests whose subject knowledge was immense and which was skillfully taught. There was a high percentage of boarders in the school and there were frequent challenges on the playground between the day boys and the boarders.

It was here that my obsession with winning the football matches during this playground time became seriously unbalanced and totally influenced my ability to learn. From 9 o'clock onwards to the time for the morning break, I would be thinking about how we could win today. I was so immersed in this that I lost all perspective of why I was in school. Prior to starting the O-level syllabus at the start of the 4th year, I had retained very little knowledge on Latin, French, Physics, Mathematics and aspects of science other than chemistry.

The end of term report came and when my father had read it he moved towards me and, without speaking pointed to the number in the class, which was 19. He then pointed to my position in the class, which was also 19. Not a word was spoken. In addition to being embarrassed, I was conscious of how much I had disappointed my parents but particularly my father.

At the start of the 4th year I began to apply the same intensity of commitment to my work as I had to the informal playground games. In the next relevant report I became 1st in the class in English literature and second in history. I cannot recall my mark in chemistry but felt confident of doing well. I had moved up from being bottom of the class to fourth place. I am convinced that it was my strong and intense focus on a new academic challenge that owed its inception to my earlier acquaintance with sporting challenge. It was too late to make amends in maths, physics and languages, which required a thorough grounding over many years. I was successful with the other subjects and able to pass the requirements for entry into teacher training college.

One of my friends at this time was Tom Foster, a day pupil, who, after the relevant training came back to the school on a permanent basis as the physical education teacher. He was an outstanding rugby player, scoring a try in the final under 18 England trial but unfortunately was not selected. He came back from the European International Catholic Student Games with a bronze medal from the hop, step and jump event. He was very unassuming and relaxed about scoring a goal in our playground encounters with the boarders, whilst I would run over to him and congratulate him in an excessively emotional way.

This rampant enthusiasm on my behalf clearly irritated some of the boarders and I felt certain that one such boarder clearly set out to injure me. The tennis ball was thrown in from the side and as I jumped up to head it, I clearly felt a foot pulling my lower leg away and I landed on my knees on the cemented playground floor. This was the same pupil who threw a cricket bat at me as I ran excitedly towards the nets claiming it was my turn in the nets. The full force of the bat hit me on my shins and to this day I cannot understand how my legs were not broken.

Despite my obvious animosity towards the pupil it did make me think about how my excessive enthusiasm for contests was irritating others and I began to rein in my enthusiasm and to be more modest in victory.

I cannot recall exactly how old I was when I decided to no longer play cricket and turn my attention to tennis but having won the under 16 event in the Carlisle municipal tournament I would have been 14-15 years old. I was already a member of the Chatsworth Lawn Tennis Club and so had a distinct advantage over those other pupils who had more restricted opportunities to practice. Nevertheless, I am convinced that my thorough grounding in cricket strokes helped me to understand and apply the principles relevant to both strokes of taking the bat/racket back, hitting through the ball and the emphasis on the follow through applicable in both games.

I cannot recall having any difficult matches in reaching the under 18 final for the second time. I had played regularly at Chatsworth L.T.C. and was used to a more competitive structure from participating in club nights; league matches and the occasional "American Tournament" staged at different clubs in the area and which invited us to join them. My school had a much greater emphasis on rugby and athletics and although some pupils played tennis it was more often in an unsupervised way. However, I remember one occasion when I was having trouble beating one of the boys from school who I had not expected to provide any real challenge. At the change over my father came up to the railings of the court and said, "Do you realise you are hitting every ball back to him? Hit it to the side and make him run." I did this and in making him run his game fell apart quite spectacularly. He no longer had the same racquet control when playing his shots and I went on to win the game quite easily.

In my introduction to the senior school running became my other great passion. I loved the feeling of exertion and being in a position to set myself new challenges as I ran along. After attending Sunday School I would run home. I ran round the rugby field once after I had my lunch and before returning to primary school. Until one day my mother said she was worried about me as I was getting too thin so I stopped doing it but I would still run home from school. On holidays at Silloth it felt magical to run along by the sea and to feel the resistance of the sand as it tried to slow you down.

In my involvement in cricket and tennis I would spend hours in the Tullie House library tracking down instructional books on how to play and how to train and practise for that activity. Running was different, or so I thought, and I just ran and ran until I was exhausted. I knew nothing about interval training, or other methods to increase your stamina or speed of running. I thought all you had to do was run regularly and in a competitive situation to get to the front and stay there!

In the evenings I would often run round the rugby field 5 times which I thought estimated a mile and I always finished with a sprint over the last 100m. I imagined that the crowd was cheering loudly as I overtook all the leading runners and crossed the finishing line first. I ran to enjoy myself but it was no basis for improving my speed over this distance. I also ran a four-mile distance 3 or 4 times a week in the same relaxed way. I ran in the Carlisle schools cross country race and finished 15th out of a field of 80 plus. My effort was a reflection of my inadequate training method.

The mile always held a fatal fascination for me and from a very early age I entered the mile race whenever I could. In my final year at school, the teachers for the first time decided to handicap the race. I had won the school cross country race easily without any significant challenge and it was decided that I was to be positioned on the starting line and all other runners were moved 30-40 metres up the track. The mile runners set off at a ridiculously slow pace and so I sprinted towards the large group and, on reaching them, ran at their pace for about 60-70 metres until I recovered my breath and then ran to the front and quickly began to move away from them. It was here that things began to go wrong.

Sports day was run on a house basis and the winning house would be the one which had acquired the most points! The boy who had won the 400metre race ran behind me and told me to slow down as it was reducing the chances of other Stafford house runners achieving relevant points. I don't think this was strictly true but I felt intimidated by him as he repeated the order several times. I slowed down considerably but still ran from the front. The race ended with a sprint over the final sixty metres and I was overtaken about ten metres from the line.

I had been clearly outwitted, unfairly I thought and I was not only disappointed but extremely annoyed. On crossing the finishing line I noticed a pair of running shoes at the side of the track and I lashed out aggressively with my foot kicking them as far as I could. In all my sporting challenges I have many times felt such disappointment but never such rage! I was my school cross country champion, my school, city and county tennis champion but none of them would ever eclipse the joy I would have felt had I crossed that line first.

Chapter Four

GETTING THE ELBOW

A Psychological Hurdle

❧ ❧ ❧

THE MOST FRIGHTENING and distressing experience I ever encountered on a tennis court was the day I had an unexpected attack of nerves. The effect was completely alien to me and as a young player who had approached each match with a real excitement for the challenge and occasion I was completely bewildered about what was happening. I was not only confused but felt real fear that such emotion could destroy my pleasure in playing.

I recognised the similarity with the fear and lack of bodily control I had felt when once attacked by an Alsatian dog. As a young pupil I attended church each Sunday and ran home from the Lowther Street Congregational Church to my home. It was a distance of about three quarters of a mile and I loved the physical exertion after a long hour sitting still!

I had been running for about 300 metres when I noticed a man walking towards me with a large Alsatian dog. I decided to ignore it and run straight past although the pavement was very narrow. I was almost level with the dog when it hurled itself at me at about chest height. It didn't actually touch me but my whole body froze rigid in terror and I felt a complete absence of any bodily control.

It was a similar situation on the court. My arm seemed locked and my legs lacked control and I was unable to do any of the normal swings of the racket which had always seemed so natural to me. I couldn't keep the ball in court for even the simplest of rallies and I remember the crowd clapping sympathetically when I eventually won a point. I had played my opponent earlier in the week in the handicap event and lost only a couple of games despite having to concede a point in all games. I was very confident I would win and would have found it inexplicable if I had thought I would lose 6-0, 6-0 to this player I had so easily beaten earlier in the week.

What had caused this attack of nerves? I remember clearly how instantly it happened. I walked on to the court and there on display at the front of the table was the large trophy for that particular event. It was the largest cup I had ever seen and I immediately felt the importance of the event. I was suddenly overwhelmed by it all. As my play disintegrated I felt the inevitability of it all. I had no "plan B "or alternative strategy. I felt completely powerless and there was nothing anyone could do to help me.

As I left the court I had to get away. I went for a walk round Keswick where the tournament took place. I was in effect running away. It was the darkest day of my life on a court both then and since. I felt strongly that I never wanted to play tennis again. Nothing could have consoled me at that time. If this was going to happen there was no point in playing again! The fear was that it was so unexpected and I was powerless to respond to what had happened. There were no sports psychologists in those days and no research material to show you the benefits of positive thinking!

Many years later I observed a student I taught "running away" and completely distraught because of what had happened on a netball court. I was driving my car along a road close to Endsleigh College, where I lectured in Physical Education. I saw this young student, Yvonne Williams, walking down the road sobbing and clearly severely distressed. I drew alongside of her to help her but as my car stopped she ran away continuing to cry and to shield herself from my observation. She was part of the netball squad which was one of the finest in the country and there was real competition for places in the team. She had been excluded for a significant match and couldn't hide her immediate disappointment. Some years later she wrote to me asking for a reference and described herself in detail implying that I may not have remembered her. How strange! I have felt her pain to this day.

My next acquaintance with such anxiety was when I was playing in the final of the County under 18 tournament. My opponent was Ian Graham who was an outstanding badminton player. He had won a national title in the all England championships and so was obviously a fit athlete and able to absorb any mental challenges irrespective of his undoubted skill at badminton. I had beaten him in the semi final of the Cumberland under 18 championships 6-2, 6-5 the previous year and so was clearly aware of having to play my best if I were to succeed again.

I was 5-0 down in the first set and was completely overwhelmed by his tactical approach. He was perilously close to the net on almost every point and volleying the ball away at a fine angle which prevented me from getting my racket on the ball. I decided to lob him and the game changed round quite dramatically. He found it difficult to maintain a rally from the back of the court and I began to have complete control in how the game developed. I lost the first set 6-3 but won the second set 6-1 and was 3-0 up and forty love on his service when he fell heavily on the court and injured his finger. I was stroking the ball consistently from one side of the court to the other when I wrong footed him and he lost his balance and fell awkwardly on the court. He left the court to receive medical attention and was at least a quarter of an hour away.

I was left to imagine what could happen. I had won 12 of the previous 13 points and it was inexplicable to assume that I might lose. But my mind began to think what if I have an attack of nerves and the game changes round for a second time!

I began to think that I would have no idea how I would feel until play resumed. However, on his return and serving at love forty down, I quickly outplayed him to take the score to 4-0 and only then could I relax knowing that I was to be free of any nervous attack. My mindset was wrong in that I waited to see what would happen and believed that I had no control of the situation.

I never experienced an attack of nerves again but was often anxious that it might happen. Late in my career at 40 years old I had reached the final of the Darlington club tournament and was particularly keen to win the singles event and maintain my record of having won the club tournament in all the places I had lived since leavings school and starting college.

I was playing a young 18 year old, Angus Allen, who was improving quickly and I knew it would be unlikely that I would have a further opportunity to take the title. I did win and he won the event for many years after proving that I was right in my prediction.

On the morning of the event I had arranged for a practice for half an hour or so to see if I was to be troubled by nerves, and if so, how I could counteract it. However I felt I was timing the ball well and began to believe, as it was, that I would be free of any problematic attack. In all these situations involving anxiety my approach was negative in not knowing what might happen rather than adopting a more positive viewpoint and mental strategy to eliminate the likelihood of it happening.

It is often not difficult to recognise an attack of nerves in your opponent and to observe the disintegration in his play. It is perfectly feasible within the rules and the spirit of the game to capitalise on such misfortune.

I have twice exploited this situation. I was playing in a veteran's over 55 match for Cumbria against Oxford and playing a singles event against Oxford's number 2 player. I won a close first set but lost the second and was slightly down in the final set. I suddenly noticed that he made some uncharacteristic errors when he was in a good position to put away a weak return of mine which had landed close to the service line. He appeared to delay his shot and then snatch at the ball and hit it into the top of the net. His body language and mumblings indicated the anxiety he was experiencing.

I began to exploit the situation and although I began to consistently win the point on such a tactic I felt sorry for the distress I caused him. A year or so later I watched him playing a match in the British Indoor event and the quality of his play was excellent and on a level far removed from that hesitant play I had exploited.

Another player who capitulated in the same way was a friend of mine, Ann Walden. Ann was a County veteran player who loved playing singles and perhaps found it difficult to find a worthwhile competitive challenge with other women players in the club. We were of a similar standard and style of play and had some wonderful competitive challenges over several years. Ann was the fittest women I ever played and we often had long rallies of twenty to thirty shots before a point was won. She was particularly skilful in dispatching any short ball for a winner on her forward side and preventing me from even getting my racket on the ball. A shot I was never able to master with such efficiency.

In the early years we played I managed to remain unbeaten despite some incredibly close encounters. Then, as she got better and I slowed down and became less mobile, the balance shifted to her winning on most occasions. We played each week and in the last six months I was unable to win a single match.

The games however were still extremely close and on this particular occasion she started making error after error on a short ball which had just cleared the net. She became flustered and nervous as I repeated the tactic which helped me to turn the match in my favour. It was clear evidence of her getting the elbow. She suddenly stopped and asked if we could stop playing and 'just hit'.

I was disappointed that she denied me the chance of winning and although I felt sorry for her obvious distress, I also thought it was a way of her meeting her demons and finding a way out. My point of view was that it was a legitimate tactic. The next week we played she began by apologising for how she had reacted.

A doctor, she lived in a large house amid beautiful and extensive gardens. At the side of the house was a child's football pitch and beyond the house and at the back were further gardens extending towards the all weather tennis court. Beyond that were fields where cattle and sheep grazed contently. It was an idyllic environment and I loved playing there. I would finish school at 4p.m. and drive the three miles to her house. They were tennis occasions I looked forward to with excitement and real pleasure and I was anxious that I had not overstepped the mark! She was too kind to let that happen and I think realised it was something she had to work on.

CHAPTER FIVE

ADOPTING REALISTIC CHALLENGES

Assessing the opposition. Understanding your own potential

❦ ❦ ❦

I T WOULD PERHAPS be best to start from the thoughts of the poet Robbie Burns. "O wad some power the giftie gie us, To see oursels as ithers see us." Translated from the Scottish tongue it means—"O would some power the gift to give us, To see ourselves as others see us."

A very common problem with some club players is they are not in tune with what is really happening. They either fully underestimate the skill of the opponent or lack clarity in understanding their own limitations in relation to their opponents' skill. I remember a club match I played in almost fifty years ago when, in a mixed doubles match, a comment was made which indicated an almost embarrassing lack of understanding about what was really happening on the court.

It was a mixed doubles match and we were 40 love up in this particular game. On three successive points I made a strong attacking shot which forced the opponent to make a weak response and the ball floated gently at a height and provided a simple opportunity for my female partner to smash the ball into the open court. It was one of those occasions when it seemed easier to return the ball into the court than out of it! All 3 smashes landed in the net as she allowed the ball to drop too low. We eventually lost the game when my wife heard a lady, who was standing by those watching the match, comment, "Howard Nixon should be dropped from this team because he cannot hold his serve."

I have found that so many people misunderstand the relevance of the serve in relation to what is really happening. Players talk endlessly about winning or losing the serve in relation to the outcome of the match. In many cases this is simply not relevant. The purpose of having a strong serve is to cause some difficulty in the opponent's return of the ball thereby providing the server with the opportunity to attack with advantage from the weak return. An ace, of course, provides the ideal response.

However, if the server is unable to cause any difficulty for the opponent in his return of shot then his service advantage is nullified. I have watched so many players play a singles match where both players had weak services and which the outcome of the match depended on their ground strokes and their rallying from the back of the court and yet still insistent that the match was won or lost on those vital service breaks! I must concede, however, that because of their belief in the serve advantage and despite their misconception of their skill input, the point is often won because of a more determined response during their service games.

One of the glaring weaknesses in my own game is my reluctance to volley and when I have opened up the court and forced my opponent wide I have been incapable of taking the ball earlier and generating a little more pace or exploit my advantage by moving forward into the volleying position. I have described elsewhere how a crucial point was lost when I had my opponent on the adjacent court when he returned the ball deep into my court and I was still unable to capitalise on his return as I remained in the same place on my side of the court.

I have played Ray Ranson, the Yorkshire number one player in his veteran age group and lost on six occasions. The first time I played him in the Doncaster Tournament I lost in the semi-final 6-2,6 4. It had rained and we played on a shale court which was his least favourite surface. The following year I played him in an earlier round and I lost 6-0, 6-1. He constantly drew me up to the net and either forced me into a volleying error or swept the ball imperiously past me. He certainly knew how to exploit weakness.

The first occasion I won the singles in the Cottingham Club tournament in Hull I won the match on a simple tactical change. My opponent was playing a serve volley game and getting far too close to the net on his advancement towards it. I then started lobbing him and he then had to scurry back to the baseline to retrieve it often not managing to do it. From then on it was a comfortable win. I have outlined in even more detail how from 5-0 down in the first set in my County under 18 singles final the game completely turned round on the same tactical change.

A tactical change is only relevant in relation to success if you have the skill to enact it. In attempting to draw your opponent up to the net to perhaps force him into a subsequent volleying situation you can get into difficulty yourself if your shot clears the net by too much and enables your opponent to play a more attacking shot which causes you difficulty. I have learned that to achieve your potential against better players it is not sufficient to just retrieve each ball and place it back into the court because they, too, can contest long rallies. You need to utilise your strengths whilst detecting any vulnerability on their behalf, which you can exploit. If a tactical change is required be sure you have the skill to carry it out.

There are times when no tactical change is necessary despite being in a losing position. In the semi-final of the Huddersfield veterans' tournament I was 5-0 down to an opponent who played an aggressive serve volley game. It had felt that I was not returning as effectively as I was capable of despite the soundness of his volleying.

My timing got better and as I began to more consistently return the ball he responded by trying to raise his game by hitting the volleys closer to the lines and with increased power. His mistakes began to multiply and the game swung in my direction and I ended up winning a close three set match.

I have played so many players over the years who have said, when I have beaten them, that I only keep the ball in the court and that if they hadn't had an uncharacteristic loss of form on that day, they wouldn't have lost. On subsequent matches the results were the same! I do move the ball around the court and force them to play a more difficult shot with which they are less competent in playing. Alternatively in their frustration of having to face a repeated return of the ball they try to hit a clean winner or some extravagant shot of which they are not capable. Of course the same thing applies to me when I play a player who can hit consistent returns but has that extra controlled attacking flair with which to achieve his victory.

I have seen so many occasions with a player playing a serve volley game when clearly unsuited to it. If it isn't working then some modification should be tried. A likely alternative would be to only approach the net when your opponent has been forced onto the defensive and, failing that, to challenge from the baseline. Either way the player needs to think about what is happening!

In one of my last appearances at Wimbledon I watched a men's singles event in the 45plus range and I could scarcely believe what I was seeing. One of the players had an impulsive desire to race to the net on every conceivable occasion. On most occasion s he was off balance as he lunged forward to play the volley which he sent well beyond the baseline. On receiving serve he instantly followed his first return to the net and repeated his mistakes. I have never seen such a predictable result from the way he played. I wondered whether he just wanted to enjoy the occasion and that the result did not matter but his response to his errors and his body language did not seem to indicate that that was so.

CHAPTER SIX

CLUB TENNIS

An essential environment for competitive challenge.

❦ ❦ ❦

Chatsworth L.T.C. Carlisle

C HATSWORTH LAWN TENNIS Club was my spiritual
home. From my bedroom window I could see who
was playing on the courts and what matches were taking
place. As a promising young player in my early teens I was
allowed to play on club nights with the older members of
the club. Club nights were Tuesday and Thursday evenings
and Saturday from 2pm onwards. Tea would be served late
afternoon and then play would continue until about 7 p.m.
in the evening. These club nights were the heart of the club
when young and old joined together and rotated round after
a set number of games. You responded to them how you
wished. One could generate a very competitive environment

if you so wished whilst others, often much older would treat it as a social occasion.

I found that sitting around and waiting for your turn to go on you inevitably focused on how points were being won, what kind of shots were the most effective and what tactical situations, if any, were utilised. I found it fascinating watching to see if players not only utilised their particular strengths but purposefully exploited the vulnerability of their opponents game often by playing to their weaker backhand or enticing them to come forward and engage in a volleying exchange. To employ their skills in the most effective way they needed to read the game and understand what was happening.

Over a period of time it was natural that the younger players like myself would improve more quickly that the older players who statistically were about 80% of the members. There were frequent comments from these older players about how much we had improved and this gave us an increased confidence in addition to the pleasure of being complemented in this way. As a young teenager my immediate target and ambition was to be selected for one of the teams. There were men's 1st. And 2nd. teams in addition to mixed doubles teams. As far as I can remember my earliest match play experience was with the mixed doubles team. This suited my style of play where the pace of the game was much slower and allowed more opportunity to exploit any tactical approach.

I loved travelling to away games and meeting new players and experiencing a different tennis environment in addition to playing on courts other than grass. I soon learnt that the ball reacted differently on varied court surfaces and that being aware of this helped in the execution of the returned shot. I once had a session with Derek Edwards, the coach of the New Blackwell club in Darlington, where I played when I was in my sixties, and was most impressed when, after returning only a few balls, he said to me "You grew up on grass courts, didn't you?" He noted that I clearly liked to strike the ball much closer to the ground delayed my shot accordingly.

My friend, Ian Harrison, and I never missed a club night in addition to playing on the courts, other than on those days. Ian was a couple of years older than me and was a better player than me, irrespective of the age difference. We would often play on the courts long after everyone had gone home and even played on some occasions in the dark. You had to listen carefully for the bounce of the ball and then chase after it.

If it rained and play was not possible we would invent the rules to a tennis or cricket game. At the side of the hut, where people changed, there was a large roller which was used extensively in maintaining the quality of the court. That would be the wicket and you would bowl underhand to the batsman who used the handle of the racket and upside down as the bat, The bowler could put spin on the ball and make it extremely difficult for the batsman to defend the wicket. If it rained there was an indoor variation of table tennis. Using the wooden square boxes which contained the tennis balls for use on club nights as our bat and building a net with the upturned boxes and finally using a table as the surface we played a variant of tennis /table-tennis. We couldn't go home without having a game of some sort!

As a young schoolboy in his early teens my goal was to be chosen for one of the teams and to eventually reach a standard which earned me selection to the men's first team. I wished to be a county player and to try and win the club singles tournament, which took place each year in the months of July and August.

Before leaving home to go to Didsbury College to train as a teacher I had played in my first County match for Cumberland and had become a member of the Chatsworth Men's team. I played in only one club tournament prior to college and thereafter one of my most satisfactory achievements has been the winning of the club tournament in each of the subsequent places I have lived.

Strangely I played practically no tennis at college in my two years there. There was one boy who had obviously played tennis before as I could tell from his shots when we knocked the ball to each other on the grass. However, he was reluctant to play a full game on the court because of his diabetes and I heard sadly from one of the lecturers that in his first year of teaching he had died.

Late in the summer term I did play one game against a North Wales county player. It was arranged through a friend of my girlfriend, Mary. One of my objectives from my time at Chatsworth was to be regarded as a County player. I lost the first two sets about 6-3, 6-3 but won the extra set we played. I felt it would not be wildly improbable that on a better day I might have been able to beat him. Being regarded as a County player gave me, a certain status, I felt it helped to increase my confidence and motivation to improve. My friend Ian Harrison joined the college in my second year but his college commitments were different from mine and I don't recall having a game against him. There was a table tennis table in one of the student common rooms and I played many times there with my friends. I played for the college football team, and even, on one occasion turned out for the rugby team, when they were short. I could handle and kick the ball competently, but was nervous about tackling an opponent. I was asked to play full back and managed to stay clear of any confrontation until the second half.

Suddenly a large player broke through the massed defence and was well clear as he ran aggressively towards me. He was an enormous size and I felt terrified, as this giant of a man ran towards the line with the clear intention of knocking me senseless. He was only a few yards away when I was just about to attempt a feeble tackle when he slipped and fell face downward on the pitch with the ball squirting from his grasp. I must have been the most relieved player of all who played in Manchester that day!

Rhos on Sea Tennis Club

Rhos on Sea tennis club is situated in a lovely part of North Wales. It is only a few miles from the popular tourist spots of Conwy and Llandudo and lies in a favourable residential area. I joined as a Country Member for the very reasonable price of 20 pounds. During the school holidays of

Easter and Summer and the half term breaks in those seasons I worked in my father in laws restaurant in Conwy. As such there were many years when I never played tennis in the long summer holidays. This limited the number of occasions I played in tournaments and restricted participation in Inter County week to only four occasions. As a young teacher with three young children I had to work to maintain our living commitments. There were no credit cards in those days! The restaurant, known as The River Grill, was exceptionally popular and it was not unusual to see queues extending back along the road a considerable distance.

In the early morning I had to deal with the arrival of fish containers from Grimsby where fish were packed tightly in ice and it left your hands feeling numb with the cold. The rest of the morning was spent with potato machines preparing the potatoes to be fried as chips. From noon onwards to nine o'clock I washed and dried the dishes, as there were no dishwashers in those days. During that long time from 12 noon to nine in the evening there was no time I could have a break. If I went to the toilet I would return to dishes piled on the floor and it was a constant battle to keep on top of it. The challenge was not unlike that of the game itself! It required stamina, concentration, emotional control and an ability to think ahead

It is easy now to understand how I completely submerged myself into Veteran Tennis as it arrived on the scene at a time which coincided with my just having reached at 45 veteran age. In my fortieth year I played in the club tournament at Rhos on Sea and won the singles event and the men's doubles with the player I had beaten in the singles. In the morning in the mixed doubles event my partner and I won through to the afternoon final which we lost in the third set and which finished around nine o clock. Excluding the morning game I had played continuously from 2 p.m. to seven o clock in the evening. It was late in that third set when I began to feel tired for the first time and which I felt caused mistakes which previously hadn't occurred throughout the day.

My singles win was I felt due to a slice of luck. I had broken the string in one of my rackets but was able to borrow a new racket from a sports shop which was strung at the exact tension I preferred. It was, however, much lighter that my broken racket. I found that it gave me the control I required but my return shots were less deep than I intended. My opponent liked to attack with a ball hit hard on the forehand side but was vulnerable to a short ball which demanded he move forward quickly.

In the many times I had played with him in club sessions I had noticed this weakness in his game and yet in preparing my approach to the game I had not intended to utilise this particular strategy. It happened accidentally but now, many years later, I realise I should have adopted it as a prominent strategy in thinking ahead about the game. He tended to scoop it up and out of play or delay his strike which caused the ball to end up in the net.

As the holder of the singles title I played in the tournament again the following year. The shale courts were very slow due to some heavy rain when I again played in the final. My opponent Andy liked to hit the ball hard particularly on the forehand side. I was two points from wining when I chose tactically to play a shot which I was never ever again tempted to repeat! After a long, grueling rally I decided to hit the ball slowly on to his favourite wing. I had thought that this sudden opportunity might cause him to be over exuberant in the acceptance of this gift and that he might, as a result, hit it long. Exactly the opposite occurred. He moved forward confidently and hit a clean winner with me unable to get my racket on the ball.

Andy went on to win the second set and we decided to play the third set on a different day because the wet weather was becoming increasingly severe. We returned to play on a day when the conditions were perfect and which encouraged a more attacking approach. I was overwhelmed by Andy's attacking approach with the ball hit early and hard. I lost the final set 6-0. He fully deserved his win.

I played in several league matches for Rhos which took place on Saturday afternoons and I loved travelling to new places and meeting fresh opposition. During the season there were some light hearted and fun open days when after about 7 games you changed partners and played the same number of games again. On one particular tournament I was intrigued by the attitude of my partner. First she told me off for not being serious enough and not trying harder to win. She was considerably older than any of the other lady players and yet she was by far the fittest.

I had my answer a few days later when I read an article about her having just been to Buckingham Palace to receive a special medal from the Queen in honour of her commitment to athletics and training women army athletes. In her own endeavours she had won a silver medal in an Olympic 800 metres track event Now I knew why she was so fit!

English Martyrs L.T.C. South Manchester

I have written elsewhere how much I enjoyed my time playing here. My first teaching post was under the Manchester Education Authority and for the next eight years all my recreational time was spent at the club. There was a wonderful family atmosphere about the place and the friends I made there are still closely in contact with me over 50 years later! The club had never won the South Manchester league and in my last year at the club we managed to win our remaining match and take the title. I remember my close friend Paul Livesey coming to talk to me just before I was collecting my things to leave for home and saying quietly how much he wanted to thank me for helping to achieve this success. It was one of those special moments.

The match almost wasn't played. The match was initially postponed because of the weather and there was a deadline for when the rearranged match had to be played. We were running out of time in doing this and faced the possibility of losing the relevant points for a win. I was with Paul, the captain, when he was explaining to me how he didn't have the phone number of the captain of the team we were due to play and didn't quite know what to do! We had been to Conwy in North Wales for the weekend and were in a petrol station getting petrol when a car drew up alongside. It was the person we needed to contact! We had bumped into each other ninety miles from home!

I didn't play often in the club tournament because of my work commitments in the cafe. I won the club singles on the four occasions I entered and on one of those years I was 0-40 down and a set and 5-4 down in an early round. I concentrated on just getting the ball back into court and I managed to claw the points back.

On my last final win I played my friend Ian Harrison who had also come to Manchester to train at Didsbury College and had joined the club. I had never beaten him other than in Handicap Events in the Cumberland Open and Nithsdale Open, Scotland and only won on this occasion because of an injury he sustained on the court.

I have to admit I was quite ruthless in making him run as much as possible. He was not able to play any point hit wide and after losing the first set I won the last two by adopting this strategy.

At Cottingham I played in the tournaments and league matches but otherwise did not involve myself very much in the social side of the club. It was my first lecturing post in Hull and I had little free time because of my commitment to take the first students through the degree course. I found I wasn't as involved in the club as much as I should have been and it clearly led to a less fulfilling experience.

New Blackwell L.T.C. Darlington

In 1975 I moved to Darlington to take up a Senior
Lectureship at Middleton St. George College of Education.
At that time there were two tennis clubs in Darlington
almost side by side and they eventually joined together to
become the New Blackwell L.T.C. I began to involve myself
more fully into club tennis again and in addition to playing
regularly on club nights I played for the first team in the local
league. However, it was only rarely that I was able to play in
the club tournament because they kept to a strict timetable
for the matches with the finals being played at a time when I
was still unable to play because of work commitments in my
father-in-law's restaurant.

My clear ambition was to win the men's singles so that I
was able to say that I had won the men's single event at the
local tennis club at each of the places I had lived apart from
Chatsworth where I didn't play beyond my school days.

The outstanding player at the club when I first joined
was Bob Severs. The mens' doubles event was organised by
placing a team player with a weaker player so that everyone
had a better chance of some success. Despite this limitation
for Bob, he had still won the men' doubles event on the
previous seven occasions; an outstanding achievement. I am
not familiar with how many singles titles he had won.

The first time we played a singles match was on a Sunday
morning when he normally preferred to play. Bob won the
first two sets and I won the next two sets. However, in my
book he had won the match because of the first consecutive

sets. I cannot recall with confidence the score in the second match but I'm sure he won again. Then the club introduced a ladder system whereby players could challenge one another and the results were recorded to decide placement on the ladder. One set was to be played. Bob won this set and at a later point in the morning we played another set which Bob also won. The psychology of playing these two sets apart in the way that it transpired was different from playing two known consecutive sets and so it did not influence my confidence that I was capable of winning a match against him.

Another factor was that the weather conditions were horrendous. There was one particular shot that Bob successfully played which indicated the extent of the wind. He had shaped to play a forehand shot when the ball suddenly turned 180 degrees. Bob then swished the racket quickly across his body and played a sliced backhand shot.

I then played him one fine summer afternoon before departing to Wales for the rest of the summer school holidays. This win gave me the confidence to know that I was capable of beating him. I was to play him three more times; in the club's final and semi final, and in the final of the town's over 45+ veteran final. In my first single's final I lost the first set, won the second but lost the final set to lose 2-1 overall. I felt I was outplayed particularly on the consistent deep balls he hit close to the baseline. The Club Secretary, who was sat in line with the base line told me that I played several out balls as in but I did not feel It influenced the outcome of the game although one might argue that had they been called out he might have reduced the subsequent length of his deeper shots to the base line thus putting me under less pressure to play my normal retrieving game. In fairness to Bob I'm not convinced this would have happened.

The last but one time we played was, in my mind, the most revealing of all because I felt prior to the game that I would win. I had just played in the Ilkley tournament and I had been playing as well as I could. I lost the first set yet I felt that I was still capable of winning if I could just cut out some of the unforced errors I played. I won the second set and was 4-2 and game point up when I had a glorious opportunity to reach 5-2. In a long rally I hit the ball deep into the backhand court and then into the forehand court. Bob struggled to reach it and scooped the ball up and it just managed to appear to clear the net. The ball was spinning and losing momentum as it travelled. I needed to reach forward and confidently punch it into the backhand court or play a short angled ball into the forehand court, but I panicked and snatched at it and it ended up in the net. How many times I have made the same mistake on such a crucial point. On the next point he injured himself stretching vigorously to retrieve the similar shot he had played just before. We did play a couple more shots but it was clear he could not continue and he had to concede the match to me.

Bob sportingly said that I would have gone on to win once I had got to 4-2 up in the final set. Whereas in the other matches I was not sure whether I would win I had thought I would win in this one. Our final encounter was in the Darlington open veterans 45+. I won 12-10 in the closest of margins. I leave the reader to decide whether I was justified in thinking that I could now beat this opponent in games ahead.

Perhaps a draw would be a fair analysis but it was certainly what sporting rivalry is all about; seeking out a challenge to satisfy the competitive need.

CHAPTER SEVEN

OTHER UNEXPECTED MOMENTS

It really did happen!

❡ ❡ ❡

NEARLY ALL WHO play regular tennis can recount occasions when something unexpected happens and which often causes some hilarity. It was a time when a French student was staying with others as part of an arrangement between my daughter's school and a school in France. My daughter along with others from her school had been to France earlier in the year and this was a time when the situation was reversed and Jean Paul was staying with us.

He was a keen tennis player and so it was not long before a game was arranged at my local tennis club. His English was not particularly good and with me being unable to speak even the most elementary French there was difficulty in understanding what each of us was trying to communicate.

He was talking to me in an animated way and I was leaning over towards him in trying to make it easier for us to understand each other as I drove along.

I turned off the main road and into the private narrow track leading towards the tennis courts. Cars are parked to the left of court 1 and beyond with the clubhouse and seating arrangements to the right. This means that any car arriving towards the parking area is clearly seen by all who are sitting there. I jumped out of the car quickly anxious to begin playing when right behind me was a police car with the officer out of his car and walking towards me as he pulled his note book and pencil from his pocket. He was clearly embarrassed by the unexpected situation he found himself in and asked sympathetically, "Didn't you see me behind you?"

I didn't look at the spectators as I walked past them on my way to the changing room. I thought he might let me off but the inevitable fine arrived a few days later!

Some years previous to this situation and on the same court 1 and during tournament week a similar embarrassing situation occurred. I was playing on court one when I felt something on my leg which was as if the lining of the lower part of my shorts had come away. I looked down and saw a pair of black knickers which had worked itself down from my pocket to the end of the shorts. There was obviously a small hole at the bottom of my shorts and during its time in the washing machine my wife's knickers had found its way into one of the pockets.

As discreetly as I could, I pulled them out of my shorts and put them in my other pocket. I never looked once at those who were watching in case of further embarrassment and to this day I still have no idea how many people saw what had happened and what their thoughts were!

Sometimes embarrassing situations can occur because of nervousness and this happened to me while playing in the National Veteran Tournament at Bournemouth. I was playing Alec Davidson, a player who has reached many national finals over the years and who has captained the England and Great Britain teams. He won the toss of who was able to decide how the game would start but before he said what he wanted to do I said "I'll take this end." I had obviously assumed he would elect to serve and said what would be my option but I had to right to say that until he confirmed what he wanted to do. Alec then said "I thought I won the toss" and, being embarrassed by the situation, I spluttered out that I had got mixed up and it was indeed his choice having won the toss.

Another embarrassed situation occurred while playing in a mixed doubles match at Rhos on Sea. My partner was a well known former Welsh International player and captain. She was much older than the rest of the players in that team yet still retained considerable respect from others. From outside the base line I scooped up a ball intended as a lob but it was well short and the opposition were able to easily win the point by hitting an unreturnable ball at my partner. As I miscued my intended lob I berated myself by shouting out aggressively "Come on" whereupon my partner turned and said, "I'm sorry" clearly implying that she thought my words were directed at her rather than myself. I was so embarrassed I couldn't reply and more than disappointed that I found

I couldn't simply state that I was shouting at myself and annoyed that I had allowed the opposition an easy return with which to win the point and that it was unreasonable to expect her to have returned the ball.

It was on these same courts at Rhos and playing in a league mixed doubles match that something strange happened and which gave me quite a fright. It was a glorious day with barely a cloud in the sky when suddenly I felt my leg go completely dead particularly from the ankle downwards. I thought it was the beginnings of some kind of stroke and wondered whether I should sit down or tell the others on the court what was happening. Fortunately the previous point had just been completed and the ball had travelled some distance from the court. This allowed me a little longer to decide what to do.

Suddenly, in the shortest time I have known, the weather dramatically changed. It clouded over in what seemed like seconds and a thunderstorm began. By the time I had reached the club house the feelings in my leg had disappeared!

In a different way it happened on the court at my club in Darlington. I was on the court and knocking up before a match was to begin. Suddenly I felt I had dislocated my ankle and I said I would not be able to play. The conditions and sudden change in the weather were similar and by the time I had gone from the courts to the nearby clubhouse my ankle had righted itself and my leg back to normal! I tell people I can forecast the weather in my bones!

CHAPTER EIGHT

SELECTED FOR SENIOR COUNTY SIDE

Limited success. Difficult adjustment from Junior to Senior level. Responding to disappointment and poor attainment. Selection issues for Hard Court Singles events.

❦ ❦ ❦

I FOUND THE ADJUSTMENT from Junior County status to Senior status difficult and I achieved only limited success. There were many reasons which contributed to this but by far the most significant reason was because of my style of play. I was reluctant to volley and my game was based on playing from the back of the court and retrieving the ball in order to put the opponent under pressure by placing the return in a section of the opponent's court which would cause difficulty. I would use the lob, drop shot and balls angled from corner to corner making it more difficult for my opponent to combat my retrieval game. Some of the biggest points played in important matches have been when I have wrong footed the player as he runs into the open court.

In doubles you are naturally forced into a pattern of play which demands a volleying response. Furthermore my smash was weak mainly through a lack of confidence rather than a poor technique and I deal with this more fully in a later chapter, but all in all I was not the ideal doubles partner. My volleying was sound in that I could control the shot and place it deep into the opponents court but it lacked pace and rarely caused difficulty, whereas an angled shot might have been the appropriate shot to play at that time. Having returned the ball I relied heavily on my partner to be involved in the winning shot.

I played four times in inter-county week and usually was the second couple. Each morning the captain gathered the team together, and I clearly remember having achieved the best results on two successive days in one particular county week.

I also played in many friendly matches against other county sides. I remember clearly my first ever match playing for Cumberland against Westmoreland. I don't ever remember Cumberland losing a match against such opposition, nevertheless I was nervous when my partner, having won the toss, decided to serve first and threw the ball to me. I threw the ball up wrongly and it was too far to the right but I nevertheless decided to continue with my service action. This caused the ball to have a pronounced slice on it and my opponent could not get his racket on it. An Ace! Unbelievable!

I did win a doubles title in an Open LTA event and my partner, Ian Harrison, and I beat an established county pair, Ferguson and Blackadder, to take the doubles title. I clearly remember my partner saying to me at 5-4 and 30 all, "If you get this point, I promise you I'll win the next point for the match". On the forehand court I returned the ball low over the net and wide enough away from the opponent at the net for him to be unable to intercept it, and as the server ran in he was forced to play a low shot down at his feet. He delayed his shot, letting the ball drop too low and he volleyed it into the net. We were Champions of our first LTA open tournament!

It was singles events, however, that I really loved. It was here that I expected to be most successful. Unfortunately, these singles matches were arranged on a friendly basis unlike now, where there is a structured singles league. The matches were arranged with teams within a reasonable travelling distance. This meant that we tended to play teams of a high calibre such as Yorkshire and West Scotland. The captain decided to play me as the number two singles player. I clearly did not deserve this ranking but it was clear to me that what the captain was doing was sacrificing my position, which was probably five or six, in order for a better player to play lower down the order and therefore have a better chance of achieving success. I was only a young schoolboy and I felt nervous about challenging this selected order, but it was something that I felt deeply disappointed about. I was consistently playing against players of a much higher ability;

however there was one occasion where I came so close to winning.

I led 4-2 in the final set and decided to try to complete the game by hitting the ball a little bit harder and by projecting the ball closer to the end line. I began to make more errors; as I hit the ball harder it seemed to suit my opponent more. From a game that I was so close to winning I found it drifting away from me because of the poor tactical change. I lost the game that I was so close to winning.

This constant occurrence of my being placed in an unreasonable position meant that not only was I bitterly disappointed but it began to sap my confidence. We played matches against Durham and Northumberland which were weaker opposition and the player playing in either fifth or sixth position for Cumberland won his match. I looked closely at the opposition he was playing and felt that I could have won that match. I felt constantly thwarted in my opportunities for success. I was disappointed but, more importantly, it did nothing for my confidence. I loved the kudos of being a county player and the increased status it brought me, but beneath this I suffered real disappointment.

CHAPTER NINE

RACQUET TECHNOLOGY

Adjusting to change; style of play: equipment choice; racquet tension.

❧ ❧ ❧

THROUGHOUT MY LONG time playing tennis I have been repeatedly amazed at how little thought players give to making decisions about the type of racquet would be most suited to them. There is the frame its self, its shape and size it addition to the string pattern and tension. Finally there should be concern about the grip size and even the composition of the handle rap.

Often at the start of a match while you are getting your racquet out of its bag or your opponent is arranging his water bottle or whatever I have noted the racket he is using and asked what string tension he has in the racquet. In my experience it is extremely rare for my opponent to give a precise figure. They usually respond by saying something like

"I asked the sports shop to string it tightly for me." I do realise that it costs extra money to experiment with different racquet string tensions but I find that a slight difference of just two pounds can make a dramatic difference to how you feel the ball on the racket.

Generally speaking a tight string tension of 30 pounds allows you to have more control in the execution of your shot where as a racquet strung with a looser string tension will allow you to more easily generate pace in your stroke but without the same control. I did once read a rather sophisticated article in a tennis magazine which suggested that playing with a high string tension and finding it gave you more control would then give you the confidence to swing more freely in your approach shot and, as such, generate increased pace.

Tennis coaches are well informed about such matters and can make shrewd judgments about which racquet will be most appropriate for you but I do feel most strongly about experimenting with varying racquet tensions and finding which suits you best! The grip size is also important and relatively easy to try out different sizes by purchasing for just a couple of pounds some new handle wraps.

In my early teens there almost every player chose either a Dunlop Maxply Fort or a Slazenger Challenge racquet as these were the prominent racquet on the market. There was a Cleves racquet but this was only rarely seen! Players like Lew Hoad and Rod Laver and the vast majority of players playing at Wimbledon used the Maxply Fort and it was also clearly the more attractive looking racquet but I often wonder whether I would have fared much better with the Slazenger Challenge racket which seemed to me a more evenly balanced racquet with less concentration of its weight in the head of the racquet.

I regret not experimenting more but it would have been ungracious not to accept the racquet which had been bought for me by my father. There is a bewildering array of racquets on the market now and a vast range of different weights and sizes. The more expensive racquets are not necessarily the best for you and it might be that the racquet that is most appropriate for you is one that is relatively cheap.

The modern racquets are now capable of generating so much pace that it is changing the nature of the game. The serve volley game is no longer applicable in combating the ferocious hitting from the baseline by the better players.

If we go back to that earlier time in the sixties we find that nearly all players wore the Green Flash tennis shoe. However the modern training shoe is a vast improvement on the canvas shoe and it provides so much support to the ankle ligaments. Again there are many different types on the market but provided one chooses the correct shoe size there is no real difficulty in deciding which you would prefer. There are even different tennis shoes for the different court surfaces!

It has taken me some time to feel relaxed about the changing colour and design of the tennis clothing but I do have to admit that it is more comfortable and more tolerant in absorbing increased sweat during raised levels of physical activity. It is not sensible to refuse to embrace the changes in racquet technology and other aspects of change which will benefit your standard of play on the court. It is tempting to reject a trial racquet which does not seem suitable for you after only a brief period of practice. I have felt you must persevere for some time before being too hasty in rejecting it. I recently looked at my old Maxply Fort racquet and couldn't believe that I ever played with it. It seemed so heavy and unwieldy and certainly wouldn't enable me to play to the level I can with my modern Dunlop racquet.

Nowadays there are special racquets for young children who are being introduced to the game at an early age. Indeed at a very young infant age it is preferable to help the child to acquire ball skills without the use of the racquet. Parents are often confused by this. It is best explained by looking at the introduction of all sports activity to very young children.

In my time at Loughborough College in the early sixties I wrote my thesis on the introduction of major games to junior school children. I argued that the elements of the structure of the game should be changed to accommodate the developmental age of the child. In soccer for instance this would include the size of the pitch, the goalposts, the type of ball and the number of children playing. Nowhere was this more apparent than in tennis. At one time tennis was taught by taking the young child on to the court with an adult racquet and attempting to play the ball across and above the net in a series of rallies. The difficulties encountered caused the child to quickly lose interest. Padder tennis emerged with its shortened court, lower net and bouncy ball which could be more easily controlled with the small wooden bats which young children could more easily manipulate. In the schools teachers began to adapt to the changes in presentation and there was an immediate skill improvement across a range of activities.

I recently watched a young coach at a tennis centre teaching a young child tennis. There was no racquet and using a large bouncy ball he was throwing it at the child for her to catch it. He was just a few paces from her but he varied the kind of throw each time. He varied the angle of the throw, its speed, the variance in its bounce and its proximity to the child and finally the differences in the timing of each throw. The child was loving it while mother fretted on the balcony because there was no racquet in sight. "That child's going to learn how to play tennis," I thought, "what a fine teacher he is."

CHAPTER TEN

ADJUSTING TO CHANGE

*Court surfaces, racket technology, scoring system, indoor centres and
coaching opportunities, tournament structure and ratings, clothing
styles and changes in footwear and braving the winter storms.*

❖ ❖ ❖

I REMEMBER CLEARLY, AS if it was yesterday, the excitement
of being chosen for the first time to play for my club,
Chatsworth against Cavendish, which was the leading club
in Carlisle. It was full of county players and provided a real
opportunity to pit your skills against them. There was a heavy
rainfall in the afternoon but in the early evening the sun
shone brightly, it was warm and a perfect condition for tennis
or so I thought. The grass was deemed unsuitable for play as
it had still not dried out; I was broken hearted.

How different fifty years later when I played in a mixed
doubles match when it rained so hard I wore my tracksuit
with the hood up, to protect myself from the raging

elements, for the entire match. This was the last league match I played in.

In the fifties the courts were predominately grass and clubs would not allow you to play on the courts when it was raining or when it had rained and the grass was still wet. As there were no indoor centres at that time it meant that the season was short for playing tennis. In about late September the nets would be taken down and there would be no play until the courts were opened for play in May the following year.

How fortunate for all that the court surface now allows play under almost all weather conditions. There have been several changes in the actual structure of the court surface from shale to carpet and recently to clay.

The materials in modern rackets including the string type permits participation in the rain. However it has not been possible to improve the structure of the ball and prevent it getting soggy and heavy when used in the rain. I have seen many players suffer injuries to the elbow and shoulder from playing in the rain. As a youngster I never played in the rain and have always found it not only difficult but strange that others now find it acceptable that rain does not restrict the opportunity to play.

It is easy to understand why clubs supported by the L.T.A. have changed the court surface away from grass. A grass court requires a full time groundsman and clubs have not been able to provide such expenditure and a grass court that has not been prepared to a high standard detracts from the pleasure of the game, as the bounce of the ball is uncertain. I find it sad that there are so many players at all levels of performance who have never experienced the joy of playing on a grass court. I know it is a romantic view but lawn tennis was meant to be played only on grass. There is an enormous aesthetic pleasure in playing on a grass court. In most situations grass courts are found in pleasant surroundings and adds to the pleasure of the occasion.

I played against Warwickshire in a County match. The grass courts were immaculate and in the background you could see the historic Warwick Castle. The river runs alongside the courts and the environment is particularly beautiful. A special moment to savour!

It would be foolish of me, however, not to recognise the enormous benefits of courts other than grass. The weather does not restrict the opportunity to play and coaching sessions can continue to take place.

This also applies to the many indoor centres where play and coaching sessions can continue throughout the year. The Chatsworth Club used to hire a coach for two evenings in the year. The coach would demonstrate to the assembled masses the tennis skills. However, despite these two luxurious sessions my skills and progress was dependent upon me going to the local library and choosing an instructional booklet on how to play. How fortunate the young tennis enthusiasts are today! They can play throughout the year and find coaching opportunities plentiful. There are so many more tournaments and the L.T.A. rating scheme helps the more competitive player to understand his level of performance in relation to other players.

The structure for veteran players with tournaments and county matches provides a wonderful opportunity for players to continue to compete with players of a similar age. As your age increases and your skill wanes there is still a thrill in the competitive challenge.

In addition to the change in court surface and the increased opportunities for indoor play and coaching opportunities, along with the tournament structure, the most remarkable change has been in the developing racket technology. As a youngster there were basically two choices. You chose a Dunlop Maxply Fort, which most of the leading players used or a Slazenger Challenge. There was the occasional player who used a Cleves racket but generally players chose either the Dunlop or Slazenger racket. The Maxply Fort had the more stylish design and seemed to generate more pace because of a weight distribution in the head of the racket. The great Lew Hoad and other Wimbledon champions played with the Maxply Fort and so this had to be the choice! The Slazenger racket was lighter and more evenly balanced and I have often thought it may have suited my game better to have chosen that racket.

Now there are a bewildering number of rackets on the market and pose a real problem in making the right choice. In choosing such a racket it is necessary to seek professional advice and to try out the racket over an extended time. Many of the mail order forms allow you to try out a racket over an extended time. I remember a leading veteran tennis player telling me that the first time he tried a particular racket he felt he played as well as he had ever played. He was jubilant until the next day when he played again with his new racket and he felt he had never played so badly! Take time in choosing your racket and seek professional advice particularly from your coach would be my advice. There are quite definitely differences in how the racket performs and it is necessary to see how this responds to your style of play. Financial constraints may limit your choice but the fact remains that certain rackets will improve your performance better than others depending upon your skill level, physique and style of play.

On a lighter note the other significant change has been in the type of clothing apparel worn. As a young player I always felt I would play better if I was smartly dressed. Tailored cream shorts were particularly elegant along with a crisply cleaned white Fred Perry shirt. I used to regularly white my Green Flash tennis shoes, which seemed to be the choice for everyone. I remember on one occasion over doing this and prompted the response from the County team captain, who was a farmer, "What have you got on those shoes, slaked lime?"

When players first started wearing navy shorts and coloured shirts I was appalled and thought I could never wear such clothing. I was over sixty years of age before I changed! However I now accept that the shirt material is lighter and more comfortable and more sweat resistant, but coloured shirts—not yet!

The improvement in the tennis shoe has been unquestionably significant. It supports the ankle and Achilles tendon and gives a better grip on all court surfaces. This was one change that came naturally to me!

CHAPTER ELEVEN

PERSONAL RIVALRIES

Attitudes in tournament and match play.

♦ ♦ ♦

THESE CAN GENERATE from a club or tournament situation or from a league match which is repeated each year. It may indicate how much you or your opponent has changed between these times. Our competitive need looks forward with relish to these encounters. Luck may be a contributory factor in providing such opportunities. This has happened to me on several holiday experiences.

My wife and I enjoyed a caravan holiday in France where among the many recreational facilities was a tennis court. Our grandson, Thomas, was with us and he was sent each morning to assess the standard of play! Many people play a recreational game of tennis on holiday and don't play again until the following year. Thomas would go scooting off on his bike each morning and report back with a usual score of

1 or 2 out of ten. However one day he raced back and in an excited way recorded a score of 9 out of 10.

I went to watch and there was a man—who clearly had ability—coaching a young girl, who I discovered later was taking part in a tournament close by. Suddenly she appeared to hurt her wrist and there was much anxious discussion about what to do. Clearly they decided to stop playing and as they collected their belongings I caught his eye and being unable to speak French I pointed at him and myself and played an imaginary serve. He seemed quite excited and I rushed off to change quickly into my tennis clothes. We were of a similar standard and had some wonderful games throughout the rest of the week. Often before I had even had breakfast the grandchildren would shout "Here's John Paul, he is rushing up to our caravan to get you on to the court."

It was clear we both shared the same passion for sport and its competitive challenge. I was slightly ahead in all our games and on the occasion of our last game he had a chance of converting a high forehand volley which would have given him a set point and taken him close to victory. However he snatched at the ball which flew beyond the lines and he swished his racquet down towards his leg indicating his frustration and disappointment. I wondered whether I should let him win when he was so close to winning but my competitive spirit steered me away from such a situation. In that short week we had become such good friends and he invited me to come and stay with him in his Paris home. It was a magical few days in which tennis again confirmed its ability to provide opportunities for enrichment of life's experiences.

A young student who worked on the site also promised me a game at the end of the week. He said he was the tournament winner at his university but because of work commitments he had not played for some time. He brought along five or six of his colleagues to watch the match! He was clearly a better player than I was and was technically correct in all his shots, however he wished to impress his friends and punched his volleys and other shots with a velocity that was not necessary. This particularly applied to his smash when he unnecessarily lost point after point through trying to smash the ball with unnecessary force.

I won the first set 6-0 and at that point his supporters left, clearly unimpressed. How little they knew! He began to play a more controlled game and began to suffer less from his long layoff. I was clearly fortunate to win the next set 7-5 and had I lost it would almost certainly have lost the final set as his play was becoming increasingly dominant. If he had thought more carefully about his approach from the beginning the outcome would have been so different.

Another game where anyone watching the first set would have would not have envisaged the outcome of the second occurred in Spain at a holiday complex.

My opponent was essentially a doubles player and he smashed and volleyed with controlled power. Thomas came down on his bike but turned and went away when I lost the first set 6-1. My return of serves became more consistent in the second set and, as he tired, errors became more plentiful and when Thomas returned again on his bike and asked the score I said it was 5-1 He went away and was surprised when I told him later that it was 5-1 to me and eventually 6-1 in the second set. My opponent then wished to finish and conceded the match to me saying that he was too exhausted to play a third set as he was only used to playing doubles matches There was only one occasion in my life when I was on the point of being unable to complete the game because of sheer exhaustion. It was in France and I had been down to the local tennis club to enquire about a game. A young 30 old teacher was keen to play the following day. It was an especially hot day and I had being having diarrhoea because of the sudden environmental change.

The first set dragged on and I led 12-11 when I began to realize that I would be unable to keep playing for much longer. I won the set on the first set point either of us had and as I walked towards the net I was thinking about what I could say. However, before I had the chance to say anything my teacher friend said he was sorry but he was unable to play any more in such intense heat and conceded the match to me. We arranged to play again but it rained heavily on that day and for some time after and so we were unable to play again.

How would these matches have turned out had I been able to play a more attacking game? [It's conceivable the results could have been quite different This is one of the fascinations of tournament play where you may come across an opponent who you have played many times. At veteran level this can often lead to the development of real friendship.

The first veteran tournament I played in I played a singles match against Bill Murfitt, a well known Lancashire veteran player. It was a long match with some rallies lasting over 50 exchanges and one in particular was well into the eighties.

I had decided to play with a lighter Prince racket rather than the heavier Wilson which I had been using. However although I had more control with the Prince racket I felt unable to put the ball away when I had opened up the court. I thought seriously about asking if I could go to my car to get my other heavier racket but I decided against it and was determined to persevere with the Prince racket which I felt would be the basis for better and more consistent performance.

The second time I played him the court situation could not have been any more different. It was on grass and quite different from the previous match on shale. Furthermore, the grass was slightly wet and the ball frequently 'died' as it landed on the court. I lost the first set 6-0 and had decided from the second set onwards to play an attacking volleying game from the net. There were times when I scraped a ball up from close to the net and ran back to the baseline as I was lobbed. From the baseline I lobbed deep to the back of the court which gave me an opportunity to race up to the net for a further volleying opportunity! However, my opponent prevailed and left me with the thoughts of how I would play him the next time we met. Bill said to me that I fully stretched him in that second set and had I won it he might well have been unable to win the final set. I fully enjoyed the game and looked forward with relish to our next encounter.

This took place one late evening in the Ilkley Tournament. There were no excuses this time and I felt I had a good chance of winning. I won the first set and felt unlucky to lose the second set on a tiebreak. I was within two points of taking the second set tie break when Bill completely miss hit a shot close to the net and the ball dribbled over the top of the net and provided him with a set point which he duly took. However I went on to win the final set 6-0 which could be attributed to some extent to his tiredness. He had entered more events than usual and had been playing in long matches before ours.

This was my first win against him but I was still left with the thought that I would have been challenged more closely had he not become embroiled in such long matches in other events in the tournament.

The following year I again had to play him in the singles event. Bill led 2 matches to one and I felt the result of this encounter would indicate a clearer picture of who was more likely to win such matches. It was a blistering hot day and I knew we would both be tested to the very limit of our fitness. At one point Bill, who had brought no water on to the court, asked if he could have some of mine. Well of course I couldn't refuse!

I can't remember whether I won in 2 or 3 sets but I do recall the match lasting an unfeasibly long time. I remember on one very long rally thinking "I'll have to concede this point otherwise I'm going to completely run myself into the ground." I decided I would just hit it to his forehand while I was at the net and this would allow him to stroke the ball past me rather than indicate to him how badly I felt. The ball came for me to play a high backhand volley and I just intended to push the ball towards him. Bill completely misread the shot and it ended up looking like a carefully disguised drop shot. He made no attempt to run for the ball and from my point of view the ball landed much shorter than I intended.

We had now played four times with each of us winning twice. A year or so later we played a fifth time. This was the most unsatisfactory match of those I had played. The first set went quickly to Bill and he won the second set and match in a tie break situation. I am well aware that on most occasions you can only play as well as your opponent allows you to. However, there are times when we are simply off form and not timing the ball as well as we are capable and this was one of those occasions. I was simply outplayed and lost to a better player on that day.

We played one final time when my restricted movement, a result of my Parkinson's illness prevented me from offering a reasonable challenge. I was unable to change direction quickly or move forward or backwards in sufficient time to get my feet into the right position to play the shot. I lost 6-0 and 6-1 and couldn't help but smile wryly at his clear intention to prevent me from winning even a game! A clear indication of our competitive need to succeed. All our games were different in that there were conditions which made victory to one of us more likely. I found the set of matches fascinating and it gave me so much pleasure in planning prior to the match and recollecting what actually happened after it. Oh how I wished our personal rivalry could have continued.

In over twenty years of playing in the veteran matches and in the different age groups of the Ilkley Tournament I reached the final on four occasions but was never able to win the event. I played in the 45+ final, the 55+ final and twice in the 60+ final and on two of these occasions lost in the final to Trevor. In the first match I lost 6-2, 6-3 and was well beaten.

The second occasion in a final I was within two points of going into a tie break situation in the second set, having lost the first but failed to secure tie break when a short ball was played which just cleared the net and died and although I reached the net in time I was unable to scoop the ball up. On the third occasion I played him he played well below his potential and I won the second set but I was under no illusion and realised that when he began to time his shots he would be able to take the initiative. I tried hard but was unable to capitalise on the set as he recovered his form and cut out the unforced errors which had crept into his game in the second set. On the fourth occasion I played him it was on an indoor court as the rain had driven us off the grass. I was disappointed in my game and I lost easily without offering any reasonable challenge.

After those matches were over, we would have a drink together in the bar and discuss the outcome of the game, the tournament happenings and more personal matters related to family life. Our friendship blossomed and each year as the tournament came round we looked forward eagerly to meeting again and to be with our other tennis friends and recollect our other veteran \ county matches which we would have played in throughout the year. Players were genuinely interested in other performances and how the year had been since they last met. It was a joy again to experience the thrill of competition and to share with others the excitement of being within that environment.

After the diagnosis of my Parkinson's disease it was a couple of years before I met Trevor again. It was at the Yorkshire Open in Doncaster and as I drove into the car park alongside the first court I noticed Trevor had seen me. I saw him put up his hand as his opponent was about to serve and he clearly asked him to hold his serve for a few moments while he welcomed me. As I got out of the car Trevor took a few steps forward towards the side netting and said how pleased he was to see me and he would have a chat later. True friendship and all evolved through exposure to the tennis situation.

It would be wrong to assume that the rewards of competitive play are only related to matches you have won or been close to winning. Over many years playing in the Yorkshire Open Veterans Tournament at Doncaster I played Ray Ranson on many occasions. Ray was generally the number one seed and justified this by consistently winning the tournament. He reached the final of the world father and son competition and lost in a close match against former Wimbledon champion John Newcome and his son. Along with his partner A.N. Other he has won a national title in a doubles event.

The first time I played him I lost 6-2 6-4 on a shale court, which he told me was not his favourite surface! On the second occasion playing on a hard court I won only one game. One year I reached the final of the 55+ event and in one of the changeovers he pointed out to me that I was striking the ball too far back in relation to my position and that I needed to strike the ball earlier for it to be more effective. It could only happen in a Veteran's Tournament!

In our last two matches against him I offered a more realistic challenge. In the National Open at Wimbledon I had a point to take me into a tie break in the opening set. As he approached the net I passed him on the backhand side but the ball just carried long. On the last occasion I played him in the Doncaster event I won the opening set in a long tie break. Despite never winning against Ray I really enjoyed all our matches and they were undoubtedly a learning experience. The competitive challenge was less to do with winning but the extent to which I could summon up enough resource to improve upon previous matches and to make it a more enjoyable experience for both of us as a result of the increased challenge.

One of most rewarding experiences is to play a match with a close friend of more or less equal ability. This was true of my friend Graham Parker. Graham's father had been playing in a match against the over 60's Cumbria side and he mentioned that his son was to take up a teaching post in Darlington and was looking for accommodation. Doug told him that I would be sure to help him if he got in contact with me. Graham phoned and he was invited to tea. He stayed for a further two years and we played almost every week.

In our first game Graham won the first two sets and, as such, the match. We played a further set, which I won and it gave me confidence that in future matches it may be that whoever won would be because of their better play on the night. After a year or so I had won a few matches more but then Graham, who had left teaching to take over the management of the Topspin Indoor Tennis Centre and who profited from increased practice improved markedly and from then on was able to win comfortably against me.

Recently, he asked me an intriguing question if, theoretically, my attacking game could challenge my defensive game, who did I think would win?

CHAPTER TWELVE

MATCH POINTS AND OTHER KEY MOMENTS

Responses to critical phases of the game.

◍ ◍ ◍

M ATCH POINT OFTEN means more than just signifying the possible end of a tennis contest and a final set tiebreak situation is the game at its most dramatic, where a match can be won or lost within the narrow range of just two points.

In such situations you realize the enormous factors impinging on that moment. Tennis is not just a game of skill involving stroke technique but is a composite of other relevant factors. The point can be lost on poor physical conditioning when you find you are unable to reach the ball in time. You may make a crucial tactical error, which aids your opponent rather than yourself. In such a tense situation you may find the pressure of the moment forces you to deny yourself a match you should have won.

Your level of concentration and a myriad of motivational factors can all have a significance influencing how you adapt to this dramatic event. In resolving such a point one can be left with a feeling of sheer exhilaration or abject despair!

Such a situation occurred for me in a County Veteran's match for Cumbria against Hereford and Worcestershire. In the earliest days of the L.T.A.'s veteran structure matches were organized on a regional basis and Cumbria were out of their depth in playing formidable players from counties such as Yorkshire and the West of Scotland, which later joined forces with other Scottish regions and represented themselves as Scotland. My first and only experience against an International side!

It was a perfect day for playing tennis. The sky was clear and it was hot without being humid: The setting was particularly attractive and there was clear space behind the base line and along the side of the court to allow retrieval from a wide ball. There could be no excuse for a less than whole-hearted commitment.

It is natural in those situations where you have never met the opponent to try and analyze his skill level by paying close attention to his play either in the knock up, or, if you are fortunate enough, in a match or practice session on an earlier occasion. I did feel I was capable of beating him and helping the team in winning sufficient rubbers to ensure victory. I won the first set without playing particularly well but began to lose ground soon after the onset of the second set. My opponent began making fewer unforced errors and also raised the level of his game through a greater emphasis on attack. More games began to slip by and he deservedly won the second set. I had played many three set matches over many years and so I was still reasonably confident of winning in that the third set allowed me a fresh start.

However, in the third set the match began to drift away from me and although I was never more than two games away I was not moving towards a winning position. It was then that information filtered back that the other rubbers had been completed and the score stood at two matches all. The outcome of our singles match would decide which team would ultimately win!

This surely was what I had been waiting for but rather than the excitement of the challenge I felt it an unexpected burden; I could so easily disappoint the other members of the team. We were all close friends and committed to doing well for our County. We clearly worked as a team together and shared each other's success and disappointments. The match continued on a similar path and I was close to losing the final set but managed to hang on and take the match into a final tiebreak. I was only a couple of points away from winning but eventually found myself match point down! How had I ever allowed myself to get into this position? There was only one answer; I had to chase down every ball as if my life depended on it. I was to concentrate with a fierce resolve and be careful to not to overreach myself by playing too close to the lines or attempting an extravagant shot.

At match point down I served a deep ball to his backhand and his return put me under no pressure and I was able to hit a deep wide ball to his backhand. I expected a return ball close to the line along the forehand court as he was fully stretched in retrieving the ball but in attempting this shot he got the angle wrong and it floated well clear of the court. I had saved a match point!

I have little recollection of how I won the next two points but I remember concentrating hard on each movement of the ball and trying to keep as calm as possible. I clearly did not attempt any extravagant attacking shot but was prepared to run and run and to get my racket on every returned ball. On winning the match on my first match point I felt a surge of unbelievable satisfaction, pride and relief from tension. Tactically, physically and emotionally I had called on every ounce of effort. I walked off the court leaving my racquets and bag behind. I didn't feel I had the strength to collect them. I had no need to rush off and tell my teammates I had won. I just wanted to enjoy that special moment when I knew I had given my very best and had been duly rewarded.

There were two occasions when I played in National Veterans Championships when both my opponent and I had a match point! I had played a qualifying match in the morning before progressing to a first round match in the afternoon. This was the only time I ever had to play two singles matches on the same day. I played P.J. Norman whose wife was one of the leading players in the country. It was a pleasure to play him, as he was such a good sportsman throughout the game.

I won the early games and quickly established a good lead. He was striking the ball well but just a fraction beyond the base line. I sensed that if he soon found his rhythm he would become a more formidable opponent and this is exactly what happened. I had won the first set and the game became more evenly balanced when I pulled a muscle in my right calf. It was painful but the real disappointment was I was limited in my movement around the court. The second set was lost but early in the final set I realized that I was "running it off" and I had regained my momentum around the court.

It was then that another unfortunate incident occurred. I was moving backwards quickly in order to smash a ball that was going well over my head. The heel of my shoe caught the metal line on the shale court and I fell over awkwardly and ended up on the court in a pile of dust! It was then that my opponent showed himself to be a true sportsman. He helped me to my feet and although the game should be continuous he in told me to take as long as I needed before starting play again. I washed my hands briefly because they were covered in sand but, despite what he said, I felt it only fair that I resumed playing as soon as possible.

I felt I could not grip the racket as comfortably as I wished but the discomfort soon moved off and advancing a few more games ahead I reached match point on my service. I was now faced with a particular dilemma. It was very windy and there was a real possibility of serving a fault on my first serves if I tried too hard; the second serve could pose the same problem. I had to make the right decision. What should I do?

I tried for an ace serve but the ball landed well beyond the service line. I nervously prepared for the second serve knowing that the strong wind would hamper my service action and could cause a double fault. I served and the ball was long; I had missed a wonderful opportunity to complete the match. We were in the third set tiebreak and it was at the point where Norman had two serves and an opportunity to capitalize on the misjudgment and loss of point which I had caused. He won the next point which took him to match point. He served and ran close to the net and I was clearly surprised as he had not been playing a serve and volley game. I slightly rushed my shot and although I passed him at the net the ball was well wide of the sideline and the match was his!

I had clearly chosen the wrong option of the type of serve to attempt. I hadn't served an ace serve throughout the entire match so why should I have expected to serve one then in the blustery wind?. The structure of my whole game is based on safety and the elimination of attacking shots that carry too high a percentage risk of failure.

This was the first time in all the years that I had played tennis that I had lost a singles match from holding a match point I had match point and what seemed like seconds later the match was lost. Unbelievable!

More surprisingly I was not as devastated as I would have expected. The way the game had unfolded and the attitude of my opponent contributed to it being a game to remember. In the early exchanges when he hadn't quite got his timing right and he was consistently striking the ball fractionally long

I was having to make difficult and spontaneous judgments in calling the ball long, he never once asked or queried the call. He reacted to his win with an air of quiet modesty but no doubt felt a glow of warm satisfaction.

The game had fluctuated from my early dominance to the game drifting away when I was injured. Then, overcoming my injury, to a fight back in a close third set. We had both held match points which meant the tenseness of the game and opportunity for either of us to win lasted right to the end. If it is possible to adhere to the principle that in a game nothing matters more than who wins but on conclusion nothing matters less than who has won, then this was it!

Within a few hours of the match my leg seized up and I was struggling to walk. The next morning it was even more painful and I was pleased that the game had concluded in the manner in which it had. I would have been unable to play had I won and denied Norman an opportunity to progress further.

To reach match point is clearly a key moment in any game but just as dramatic can be a situation which with hindsight was a determining factor in how the game reached its conclusion. In the early sixties when I began teaching in Manchester I played my tennis at a small Catholic tennis club in South Manchester known as the English Martyrs Club. I was the first non-catholic ever to be admitted to the club. My wife and I both had been to Independent fee paying Catholic schools and my wife, Mary, started her teaching career in a Catholic school in Manchester. A Father Guerin, later to become Monsignor Guerin, had an active role in the school.

He was a keen tennis player and it was not long before Mary had arranged a game for us. It was his influence that enabled me to become members at the English Martyrs Club. He was a good player and we had many enjoyable matches and although I never lost a game to him we always enjoyed our rivalry.

In my time in South Manchester I had never lost a singles match and had won the Club Singles on four occasions. In a cup match I had to play a player who was regarded by many as the outstanding player in the league. For some reason he had a break from the game and had just started playing again. I cannot recall his name, it is so long ago but what happened is imprinted on my brain!

There was a wonderful family atmosphere in the club and many people who played little or even no tennis came in the evenings to relax and share the convivial and warm friendships of others. I loved the challenge of this match against A N Other who no one could recall ever having been beaten in the South Manchester league or cup matches. I played as well as I was capable of and led by a set, four two in games and forty love on his service when something occurred which has haunted me for the rest of my playing career. At forty love down on his service he appeared to slam the ball in frustration and the ball whizzed past me and landed, I thought, fractionally over the base line. The game was played on court one very close to the railings which separated the spectators from the court. I was conscious that there were those in the crowd who were looking directly along the base line. I didn't call the ball out as I was nervous about making a wrong call. I also thought that there was every likelihood that he would not win three points on the run and that the outcome of the game would be mine.

How wrong I was! I became unsettled because of my lack of confidence in calling the ball how I saw it. My disappointment was even more acute when after the game many people confirmed that the ball was indeed out. Suddenly I was only 4-3 up instead of 5-2 with my service to come. I couldn't stop dwelling on what had happened and the game drifted away from me and I lost a match which at the time of the incident looked extremely unlikely. There was no doubt in my mind that the particular erroneous call I had made led from an almost certain victory to that of an undeserved defeat.

From that time onwards I became more anxious of possible errors of judgment and being perceived as dishonest. At times I dwelt on it so often that it began to spoil my enjoyment of the game. Sportsmanship had always been something that I felt was fundamental to sport and in individual encounters, such as singles in tennis. The game could not proceed satisfactorily unless both players had confidence in their ability to call correctly. My unbeaten record was gone and a new anxiety had revealed itself, but it could all have been so different.

Matches which involve winning from match point down or forfeiting the opportunity to win from a lost match point are indeed times when your full resources are called into play. But getting within two points of winning can be equally dramatic or a point played much earlier in the game which indicated a change of tactic.

In my first appearance in the National Veteran Clay Court Championships at Bournemouth I was a drawn against a seasoned veteran player, Charles Trippe, who in the past was seeded in the singles event. I was two points from winning the match when he approached the net and challenged me to pass him. I played a backhand cross court shot which he failed to get his racquet on but the ball landed just over the side line and as he raised his game I knew my chance had gone! My opponent Charles became Chairman of the All England Club the following year and I was pleased to see him stepping out with other dignitaries on to the Centre Court on Finals Day at Wimbledon.

On one of my playing appearances at Wimbledon in the National Veterans event I was asked to play in the qualifying event. I was pleased at this because it gave me an opportunity, if I won, to justify my inclusion in the main event. I wanted to feel that I deserved to be amongst those other players who had reached, in the eyes of the committee, the required level of performance.

I played Jim Goodman and was two points from winning when I hit a deep ball into his backhand corner and from his position wide on the forehand court where he had to run and control the return shot I felt quite confident of successfully winning the point. He returned the ball faster than I had anticipated but it was high over the net and I volleyed it cleanly but too close to the side line. He was beaten but the ball had landed just beyond the sideline and my chance of a match point had disappeared. Why had I gone for a shot so close to the line when a more careful shot well within the side line, would, I believe, have been a better option. The game eventually concluded in a tiebreak, which I lost easily after I had long realized that my chance had gone!

The following year I won through the qualifying event, and, even achieved greater satisfaction when in a later year having been accepted straight into the main draw I was drawn to play a qualifier against whom I won. My opponent Knight had an excellent first serve and he dominated the early part of the game through an excellent serve followed by a winning volley. Suddenly he had trouble with his first serve and he began to lose confidence in it. He stopped approaching the net and I began to change the course of the game through rallying from the baseline. The game changed not so much on my tactical approach but through his inability to ascertain what had caused such a change of fortune considering his early dominance.

My mind drifted to the similarity of situations we all experience in life. The ability to recognize what is happening and to learn from your mistakes. People of my generation lived in a much stricter domestic environment. My father was especially strict at times bordering, I felt, on unreasonableness, but I know he had my best interests at heart. He never discussed things with me but was sure that what had been decided was in my best interests.

One evening he told me to go and comb my hair and he was going to take me somewhere. I got in the car and had no idea what was in store for me. He drove into this large enclosure that was surrounded by trees and many fields. The building was old and enormously high and it looked like some orphanage. I noticed a boy about fifteen years old doing some gardening close to the building. On entering the building we were welcomed by a priest, Father O'Driscol, who was the Headmaster of the school. He took us to his study and asked me to read a passage from a book. I was a fluent reader and knew he was satisfied with how I read. However, before any further conversation I started to cry. It was then that he asked me to stop reading. Neither of them could possibly have known why I cried. It was clear I was to start a new school and this would mean that I was unable to represent my primary school in the Inter School Sports at the Carlisle United ground. This had meant everything to me and it was to be taken away. I was devastated.

Nowadays parents talk much more openly to their children and discuss with them more intimate aspects of their interests, desires and fears. It seems more profitable to learn from your mistakes and improve our relationships with others. How I wish this could happen more frequently on the tennis court; so often situations occur which are telling and warning us to take note and learn from the experience so that we can utilize that on a future occurrence. It could mean the difference between success and failure, between winning and losing!

There are aspects of the game that warn us that we need to improve on a particular skill, but by far the most frustrating thing is when we have the ability to utilize a particular skill but don't apply it at the appropriate time.

Such a situation occurred in one of my other matches in the Veterans competition at Wimbledon.

My opponent R.J. Moore played a very similar game to myself and it took some time for me to adapt to his retrieving skills. I have been beaten easily by players who strike the ball hard or those who through a more advanced skill take the ball early and put one under immediate pressure. Peter, however, not only played a very safe game with few errors but also was able to retrieve the ball from almost impossible situations.

There was one particular rally whereby he ended up on the adjacent court and the ball had been returned directly to me; it appeared almost impossible not to win the point! I took a long time before returning the ball into court concentrating on how carefully I struck the ball and guiding it safely into the empty court. He had seen how slowly I was to return the ball and had rushed back to put the ball back into play and eventually win the ensuing rally. It was a noble effort but by playing the ball a fraction earlier it would undoubtedly have been my point. Failure to learn from this occurrence was, I believe, to cost me the victory I could have had.

It took me a while to come to terms with his style of play and I found myself 5-0 down in the first set. However I battled hard and fought back to 5-4 down and had a key point to equalize the score for 5 all. I was absolutely convinced that if I could get the next point it would alter the balance of the game and I would go on to win. I was able to stretch him wide on to the forehand side of his court and he returned poorly with the ball floating well over the net on my forehand side and providing an easy volley into the gaping hole on the court.

However, I hadn't learned from my earlier mistake. I delayed and delayed and delayed before nursing the ball into the open space. Peter flung himself across the court and strained to get his racquet on the ball. He just reached it and the ball flew off his racquet and took an acute angle across the court and landed exactly on the sideline. It was an incredible retrieval, but one he had done before and on a point that should so easily have been mine. I had the skill to win the point but had not learned from my earlier mistake. Such unnecessary misjudgment left me feeling quite forlorn. I lost the set I'm sure I could have won and gone on to complete a victory. I managed to eventually take the match into a third set but the inability to win that crucial point played on my mind for the rest of the match and I felt it inevitable that I would eventually lose. How often have we made the same mistakes in life

A game which should have made so much to me was in fact a slight disappointment. I played P. Perera in a singles round in the National Championships at Wimbledon. The following year he won the Men's' Doubles title in the same age group in which we played. He was recognized as an outstanding player at national level and so it would be a particular significant win. I lost the first set without really imposing any significant challenge to him but began to make more of an impact in the second set. He was returning the ball high over the net on his service return and I was moving in quickly to the net to successfully volley the ball away for a winner. However at 5-4 in the second set he reached match point and after a short rally he moved into the net and had an easy chance of putting the ball away for a winner.

I had reached desperately to return the ball from a position well wide in the forehand court and had sent the ball invitingly for him to volley his backhand shot into the open area on the backhand side of my court. I immediately turned and began running to the side of the court in anticipation of his projected shot. At the last second he changed the angle of his racquet and volleyed into my forehand court in his attempt to "wrong foot me." I had saved a match point as the ball carried long. This galvanized me into an even greater effort and having taken the game into a tiebreak which I eventually won I felt I had a good chance of achieving a significant scalp!

However it quickly became apparent to me that I was out of my depth in my ability to force the issue. He had raised his game to a level where I could no longer compete. He was unaware how I felt but I wondered whether he was just using me as a practice session and that he had the ability, whenever he wished to dictate the outcome of the match. Somehow the pressure eased off and from six all in the final set we went into the tiebreak routine. I managed to establish a quick advantage but was surprised when he asked me to confirm the score. Occasionally after long rallies you can forget the score but this seemed unlikely in the importance of a tiebreak, which would determine the outcome of the match. I reached match point and was determined to try and win this vital point on the strength of my ability rather than an unforced error from my opponent.

I served a good serve wide to his backhand and he mistimed his sliced return and the ball floated back close to the net on my backhand side. I had anticipated the flight of the ball and was quickly up to the net and felt very confident of judging the bounce of the ball and stroking it deep into his forehand corner as he remained stranded on the opposite side of the court.

I felt quite devastated when I was unable to do this. His mistimed backhand slice had caused the ball to spin violently and as it landed and hardly moved from the floor I was unable to get my racquet on it. He held up his hand and apologized but it was little consolation to me in that I had deserved the point!

I had a further match point and after a brief rally he sliced a backhand shot low into the bottom of the net. I had gone on to win a match from match point down against a player of exceptional talent and yet I was by no means overjoyed. The match finished very late and everyone seemed to have gone home when we returned to the Referee's Table and Alan Mills was waiting for us. They clearly knew one another well and I heard my opponent say that he used his singles participation as a warm up for his preferred doubles events. Did this mean that he was not fully committed to winning our match? I'm not sure but there was clearly a doubt in my mind, which had prevented me from fully enjoying the match. Was it a hollow victory? I will never know! The real joy of competition particularly in close encounters is when both participants are striving to produce their very best and the harder the struggle the greater the reward. As in life the real joy is in coming as close to your potential as possible. I am reminded of the words of the poet Browning whose word ring true:

> "To man, propose this test—
> Thy body at its best,
> How far can that project thy soul on its lone way?"

CHAPTER THIRTEEN

WELL WHOSE POINT IS IT?

Agreeing to share a moral responsibility in confirming the score.
Resolving difficult situations.

❧ ❧ ❧

I N DECIDING THE title for this book I was finding it difficult
to establish the correct choice of words. The competitive
challenge and subsequent response was important but equally
I wanted to emphasise the moral ingredient in how I and
others reacted to situations which clearly tested the integrity
of the player. I thought of calling it "The tennis court a
microcosm of life or "The vicissitudes of life revealed on the
tennis court."

How we react on the court tells us much about
ourselves. It is helpful if we consider why rules, in any sport
are established. They are there to provide a basis for fair and
honest play. When football was first introduced there was
no penalty rule for an indiscretion in the penalty area. It

was considered unthinkable that anyone would deliberately foul an opponent! How things have changed. Games which evolved later in history had a tighter structure for penalising unfair play. It is clearly apparent that some of our major sports are in need of further rule changes to regulate for situations where an unfair advantage is manipulated by unscrupulous means. It is my belief that Governing Bodies are reluctant to such rule change because it would reveal that all is not well! It is not difficult to recognise that the difference between the amateur, Corinthian ethos and professional sport has widened significantly along its moral pathway.

In tennis I am not against the need to obey the rules but I think it is tolerable that two particular rules can be interpreted with a degree of laxity. If a ball is struck which is going well outside the court and it strikes the opponent the point is lost.

I was playing in the Indoor Championships when I mishit a shot which was caught by my opponent, who was standing well outside the baseline. It so happened that just at that moment an L.T.A. official was walking by the court who shouted to my opponent, "If I were Howard I would claim that point!" I had no intention of doing so.

The rule was clearly designed to prevent the player misjudging the situation where a ball which appeared to be going beyond the line was blown back into court. I have seen players jump up with their racket to catch a ball destined to land beyond the outside netting of the court. Is this really such a crime?

Another rule which I feel the amateur player can adopt a more lenient view about is foot faulting. I do very much understand how some players would be fiercely opposed to my thoughts on this matter. The rule was clearly designed to stop players gaining an advantage by advancing to the net quickly through a serve volley approach. It is rare to see this sequence of movement in the average club session and so has no significant appeal. I have seen club members apoplectic with rage because some player is foot-faulting when his foot has touched the line as he gently pushes the ball into court.

The real problem when you have not got an umpire is who is going to decide that a foot-fault has occurred. The players in the receiver court are too distant from the base line to accurately confirm the fault. I think it is important to point out to the opposition that a foot fault is occurring and hope that then and in future the player will work on eliminating the foot fault. It is essential that foot-faults are called and accepted by the server when an umpire is used. Without an umpire the server can call a foot-fault against himself but I have never seen this occur. So let's work together to help players to overcome this transgression, but please no hysteria!

In a county veterans match for Cumbria against Warwickshire one of their players was injured very soon after the start of the match and was unable to play any further. A replacement was sent for and arrived. This was against the rules in that the team had to declare its players shortly before the match commenced. Doug Popper the Cumbria captain ignored the rule and the game continued in an uninterrupted way where all players had a thoroughly enjoyable game. A fine and charitable response, I thought, but against the rules!

If we accept a degree of flexibility with regards to some of rules whilst playing club tennis there still exists a relevant moral framework within which we need to adhere. I am reminded of my old school motto at Austin Friars School in Carlisle. "In omnibus caritas"—in all things charity. It is taken from the words of St. Augustine:

In things essential let there be unity
In things doubtful let there be liberty
But in all things charity

It is certainly essential to know the rules and to keep the score. I played in a match for Cottingham in a Yorkshire league match when after successfully converting the match point for a winner we moved towards the net to shake hands with our opponents. They were clearly stunned in that they thought the match now stood at one set all. It was clear from their reaction that they genuinely thought we had made a miscalculation.

I remember thinking it strange that no one was confirming the score as the match moved on. The four players were all engrossed in concentration as the match proceeded and assumed there was no discrepancy with regard to knowing the score. There was a protracted discussion about each of our service games but to no avail! The only thing we could do was to play a final set, which we lost.

On the second occasion when I won the Over 55,s in the Yorkshire Open at Doncaster my opponent, Bob Oldroyd, who I had played so many times, disagreed with what I thought was the score in the early few games of the final set. He allowed the score to stand in my favour, although he was clearly unhappy about it. I did win the final set 6-3, which suggested to me, that had the score been reversed in his favour at that time, I would probably have still won, but of course I could never be sure about that and it clearly dented my pleasure in winning the event for the second time. In the many times that we played in Wales, on my holidays there, he was more consistent than I in remembering the score, but on this one occasion I felt he was wrong.

In addition to keeping the score it is also essential that during the course of the game the players are familiar with the rules. My friend, Graham Parker, who plays for Thirsk, told me of an incident when playing indoors where the first point was concluded when one of the opponent players hit the roof with a miscued shot. They then thought they were entitled to a let service. There was a heated discussion before play resumed some forty minutes later. There are rules which relate to obscure situations and players need to be aware of them.

In a club night at the Topspin Tennis Centre I was playing in a doubles match when I was caught out of position and vulnerable to a passing shot from a ball which had just cleared the net. I feinted to move left leaving an even more opportune moment for the opponent to pass me and then moved quickly back as he struck the ball directly to me and I was able to return the ball for a winner. At first my opponent said that it was against the rules what I had done and then when he was told it was not so, he felt that at the very least it was unsporting. In tempting him to play the return I wished him to was neither against the rules or unsporting, it was a successful tactical approach.

The real difficulty in playing without an umpire is deciding what to do in those situations where neither yourself or your opponent is sure about whether the ball was in or not. The rules say that if you are not completely certain about a difficult call on your side then you must award the point to your opponent. This can occur many times when two players are evenly matched and the ball is being played consistently to the lines when the full width and length of the court is being exploited. It is common for players to agree to a let in such circumstances although this can be overplayed.

It is rare to come across a player who is deliberately cheating and in most situations what has occurred is an error of misjudgment. However I have been aware of a player, who feels an injustice has occurred, who then decides to pinch a point back in the next close call.

I was playing in the semi-final of a doubles event at my club in Darlington when my partner called a ball out that one of the opposition players felt was a wrong call. I was unable to help because at that particular moment I was not watching directly as he played the ball. After a heated discussion my partner insisted on his call being correct. In the following game I served an ace to the forehand court and the ball had landed well inside the service and side line.

The opposition player who had disputed the previous call called the ball out and he knew by my reaction and the way that I looked at him that I knew what he had done. When we changed ends a point or two later he said to me as I walked past him, "Well your partner made a bad call in the previous game." I never spoke to him about the incident but he clearly recognised that I strongly disproved his action.

Apart from being dishonest one can never right such a situation by appearing to balance the error. Each point in any game has its own particular psychological impact and losing or gaining a point through such manipulation is not the answer. In a Darlington match the reverse situation occurred. The opponent felt that his partner had made a wrong call in claiming a particular point, so when he received the next ball he clearly appeared to play the ball into the net. He was trying to right the error but without any meaningful effect. I was also conscious of the fact that it seemed to affect the balance of the remaining game.

The first time I ever game across blatant cheating was when I was a young schoolboy playing in an American tournament. This is where you swop partners after so many games and the winner at the end of the day is the player who has won the most games. It is a fun event and used to encourage those players in the club who didn't normally play in matches or tournaments at the club. However, I took it seriously and had won the American Tournament at the Cavendish and Chatsworth clubs. The only other club in

Carlisle was at Eden Lawn and I was trying for the Grand Slam! In my half of the draw I tied with the same number of games as another player and we had to spin to see who went into the final. The other player, a senior figure in the club asked me to call and after adjusting his racket he threw it so only one revolution of the racket occurred and it landed to his favour. I hadn't the confidence to tell him how I felt but I was shaken by his dishonesty. It didn't help further when he went on to win the tournament.

Another discomforting feature is when an opposition player is constantly querying your call to the extent of making you nervous about your own judgment. This occurred in the semi-final of a doubles match at Rhos-on-Sea tennis club. One of the player was demanding a let on almost every close call that we made to our advantage. We were leading 5-3 in a tie break when this particular player hit the ball wide. There was not the slightest doubt in my mind that the point was ours. In order to avoid any challenge from him I said to my partner, "Well it was out wasn't it?" To my horror he said "I didn't see it." The opponent quickly said that if he wasn't sure we need to replay the point. I should have demanded that the point was ours because I had the right to call on my side. My partner had said he didn't see it because he wasn't looking in that direction not because he wasn't sure about his judgment. I was so annoyed about what had happened as I felt it completely unfair that we had been challenged in that way. We eventually lost the tie break and although we won the second set I never really recovered my composure and we went on to lose the match in the final set. His behaviour was not against the rules but it was manifestly unfair and certainly well removed from the spirit of the game.

How different from when I achieved my first victory in the Veterans event at Wimbledon. My opponent a Mr. R.Chapman, who I believe was the captain of the Cornwall Veterans team overruled some of the calls I made on my side of the court when I felt his return was good. He insisted that his ball was out and awarded the points to me. A similar situation occurred in a match I played against the Oxford Veterans team. At set point down in the first set I passed my opponent at the net as he advanced towards it but the ball was just wide and I had lost the first set.

My opponent, who's call it was, said that he wasn't sure and looked to me to decide who had won the point. I was pleased to help him accept the point. Paul Ranson, the number one singles player in the Yorkshire Over 55 Veterans team, and who I played on six occasions was another player who overruled some of my calls and awarded the point to me. It is my experience that Veteran players are just so pleased to be playing and enjoying the adrenalin of competitive play. They know that any unfair advantage given either to themselves or their opponent detracts from the joy of participation.

Nearly all who play regular tennis can recount occasions when something unexpected happens and which often causes some hilarity. In my case it was a time when a French student was staying with others as part of an arrangement between my daughter's school and a school in France. My daughter along with others from her school had been to France earlier in the year and this was a time when situation was reversed and Jean Paul was staying with us.

He was a keen tennis player and so it was not long before a game was arranged at my local tennis club. His English was not particularly good and with me being unable to speak even the most elementary French there was difficulty in understanding what each of us was trying to communicate. He was talking to me in an animated way and I was leaning over towards him in trying to make it easier for us to understand each other as I drove along.

I turned off the main road and into the private narrow track leading towards the tennis courts. Cars are parked to the left of court 1 and beyond with the clubhouse and seating arrangements to the right. This means that any car arriving towards the parking area is clearly seen by all who are sitting there. I jumped out of the car quickly anxious to begin playing when right behind me was a police car with the officer out of his car and walking towards me as he pulled his note book and pencil from his pocket. He was clearly embarrassed by the unexpected situation he found himself in and asked sympathetically, "Didn't you see me behind you?

I didn't look at the spectators as I walked past them on my way to the changing room. I thought he might let me off but the inevitable fine arrived a few days later!

Some years previous to this situation and on the same court 1 and during tournament week a similar embarrassing situation occurred. I was playing on court one when I felt something on my leg which was as if the lining of the lower part of my shorts had come away. I looked down and saw a pair of black knickers which had worked itself down from my pocket to the end of the shorts. There was obviously a small hole at the bottom of my short and during its time in the washing machine my wife's knickers had found its way into one of the pockets.

As discreetly as I could I pulled them out of my shorts and put them in my other pocket. I never looked once at those who were watching in case of further embarrassment and to this day I still have no idea how many people saw what had happened and what their thoughts were!

Sometimes embarrassing situations can occur because of nervousness and this happened to me while playing in the National Veteran Tournament at Bournemouth. I was playing Alec Davidson, a player who has reached many national finals over the years and who has captained the England and Great Britain teams. He won the toss of who was able to decide how the game would start but before he said what he wanted to do I said "I'll take this end." I had obviously assumed he would elect to serve and said what would be my option but I had to right to say that until he confirmed what he wanted to do. Alec then said "I thought I won the toss" and, being embarrassed by the situation, I spluttered out that I had got mixed up and it was indeed his choice having won the toss.

Another embarrassing situation occurred while playing in a mixed doubles match at Rhos on Sea. My partner was a well known former Welsh International player and captain. She was much older than the rest of the players in that team yet still retained considerable respect from others. From outside the base line I scooped up a ball intended as a lob but it was well short and the opposition were able to easily win the point by hitting an unreturnable ball at my partner. As I miscued my intended lob I berated myself by shouting out aggressively "Come on" whereupon my partner turned and said, "I'm sorry" clearly implying that she thought my words were directed at her rather than myself. I was so embarrassed I couldn't reply and more than disappointed that I found I couldn't simply state that I was shouting at myself and annoyed that I had allowed the opposition an easy return with which to win the point and which it was unreasonable to expect my partner to have returned the ball.

It was on these same courts at Rhos and playing in a league mixed doubles match that something strange happened and which gave me quite a fright. It was a glorious day with barely a cloud in the sky when suddenly I felt my leg go completely dead particularly from the ankle downwards. I thought it was the beginnings of some kind of stroke and wondered whether I should sit down or tell the others on the court what was happening. Fortunately, the previous point had just ended and the ball had travelled some distance from the court. This allowed me a little longer to decide what to do.

Suddenly in the shortest time I have known the weather dramatically changed. It clouded over in what seemed like seconds and a thunderstorm began. By the time I had reached the club house the feelings in my leg had disappeared!

In a different way it happened on the court at my club in Darlington. I was on the court and knocking up before a match was to begin. Suddenly I felt I had dislocated my ankle and I said I would not be able to play. The conditions and sudden change in the weather were similar and by the time I had gone from the courts to the nearby clubhouse my ankle had righted itself and my leg back to normal! I tell people I can forecast the weather in my bones!

CHAPTER FOURTEEN

RESTRICTIONS OF AGE, INJURIES AND ILL-HEALTH

Onset of Parkinson's Disease, An Uncertain Future. a
Re-adjustment to a Competitive Need

❧ ❧ ❧

I HAVE ARGUED THAT age is less of a concern in tennis than in other sports because of the opportunity to compete with players within a five year age range. Of course this does not apply to club matches you may have been chosen to play in or rather not chosen because of the improvement in the play of younger players. It is important to be realistic about this and set yourself a more realistic target which you hope to achieve.

Injuries are another factor which can curtail your ability to play to the level of which you are capable. I tore the rotator cuff in my shoulder playing tennis over an extended period of time. I was playing the very next day and could play ground shots without any discomfort but to serve was extremely painful and to volley was not quite as bad but, nevertheless it still hurt. It was almost a year before the pain disappeared in my shoulder. The most noticeable effect was that it reduced the effect of the throwing action in the serve.

The most severe injury I had was when I broke my scapula bone in my back. I had just bought a new pair of tennis shoes which gripped firmly on the court when I wished to slow or change direction. I ran hard to reach a drop; shot and when I checked my run I somersaulted and hit the ground with some force. I had got up early on a Saturday morning and we were the only ones on the court. My tennis partner was unaware of how badly I was injured and soon left for home. I drove myself to the hospital in Llandudno and it was one of the most difficult journeys ever. I couldn't use my left arm at all and had to steer, change gear and carry out any other operation by only using my right hand.

The nurse came to tell me that I was very fortunate because I was about to be treated by a very famous person who had just been awarded an O.B.E. from the Queen. The doctor came and I had no doubt that I had seen her many times before but I couldn't remember where! I was going to ask her if I had played tennis her with some time but my mind was diverted to what she had to say about the x-ray which clearly showed I had broken my scapula.

It was some days later when I suddenly remembered who she was. She was the brave doctor who refused to leave her hospital in Beirut, despite government insistence, so that she could continue to look after her patients when the bombing was at its most punishing. Her picture had constantly appeared on the front pages of the national newspapers.

The most recent injury was when I was playing in the Huddersfield Tournament and I ran into the fence and broke two ribs. I was playing Bob Oldroyd who I have played so many times before. He was well up in the first set at about 4-1 when I won a few vital points which helped me to keep fighting for a set, which had the point been lost at 4-1 and game point it was certain that I would have lost that first set. However the balance of the game shifted and I won that first set. The second set seemed to be following a reverse pattern to that of the first. I was about 4-1 up in the second set when he won two consecutive games to get to 4-3. I was desperately keen not to let the set slip away. I lunged excessively to reach a really wide ball which had taken me right outside of the tramlines. I crashed into the side netting and hit an iron fence with some force. I broke two ribs and was in some considerable pain. I tried to play a few points but it clearly became obvious that I could not continue. Bob sportingly said that if I thought I could recover to play again the next day he would concede the match to me because he felt I was in a winning position.

One or two persons have said to me that in sustaining such an injury I could probably gain some compensation from the club because they hadn't informed me of this particular accident spot. How little these people understand me! The club had invited me to enjoy the pleasure of a veteran's tournament, members had given up their free time to help in all those many ways which are required for the events to run smoothly; once again I was in a place among friends and loving the competitive environment of challenging tennis matches.

The best advice I had was from my doubles partner, Youseff Khan. When you are in a place where you have never played on those courts before have a look round and see if there are any structural parts such as fencing which could cause you a problem if you are not careful.

Sometime later, I started to have problems with my right leg towards the end of a long game. If I played a long three set match I began to feel discomfort in my right leg as the third set approached. It is difficult to describe the exact feeling as it wasn't really painful but more a sense of being restricted in my movement rather like a recurrence of an old injury. It was not related to a feeling of tiredness but simply the onset of a muscular change which was affecting my speed around the court. I was convinced that it was the beginnings of a hip problem which would gradually get worse and so I decided to consult a physiotherapist.

After an initial diagnosis, I was told that the problem was in my lower back where some abnormality was affecting the transmission of nerve impulses down my right leg. It was decided that I needed to have regular massage on my back and leg and that in time the problem would be alleviated. I continued to play tennis and went weekly for my physiotherapy treatment. However, after almost a years treatment here was no significant improvement in my condition and I ceased going to the physiotherapist.

At the same time I began to have problems which were clearly related to the nervous system. One night at about three in the morning I woke up and felt frightened with an intensity I had never experienced before. I had not been dreaming and was not aware of having had a nightmare. There was no logical explanation of why I was so frightened. I woke my wife, Mary, up and said I didn't know what was happening to me and explained how frightened I was. Mary went downstairs and brought up a cup of tea and I began to feel much better and easily fell asleep again.

Looking back on how things were I realised there was another indication of a change in my neuromuscular system which puzzled me at the time and which only later began to make sense.

It was the end of the summer term and the school arranged a rounders match between the top class and the teachers. I was positioned exactly where the ball was most likely to be hit and about 15metres from the batting area. At the very first ball the batsman hit the ball directly to me and as the ball looped towards me it was the simplest of catches. Inexplicably I dropped it much to the amusement of the children.

Normally when a mistake is made in games you can analyse the situation and understand what aspect of the skill had been at fault or neglected. However hard I tried I could not fathom out what had gone wrong. I had watched the ball carefully and was positioned perfectly to take the catch; nothing in my path affected me from seeing the ball clearly and I was very confident of catching the ball. I felt neither nervous nor overconfident which might have caused a careless response. Yes, I dropped it and there was no explanation of why it happened!

There were other indications that all was not well and which eventually caused me to seek help. For some time I had taught at Red House School, Stockton as a supply teacher and I loved being there. It was an Independent school, similar to the one I had been educated in and I immediately felt at home. Over a seven-year period I was almost continually in the school. I covered two full term absences several half term covers or thereabouts and many day or two/three day covers; whenever a teacher was off, I was sent for! I was excited whenever the phone went about seven in the morning when Colin, the Deputy Head, would begin by saying: "I need you today" I mention this in detail because there was no need for me ever to feel nervous whilst I was there. I used to arrive before 8.30 a.m. so I could familiarise myself with the day's work and then have a cup of tea and chat with my friends in the staff room. However I began to feel nervous and stressed at this time when there was no need for me to have reacted in this way.

Then on one particular day I realised it could no longer be ignored! We sat down with the children in having our lunch and it was always an enjoyable occasion. The food was excellent and there was always some amusing tale about what had occurred during the morning session. I suddenly realised that I didn't want to eat and I had no appetite whatsoever. I had to force myself to eat and was embarrassed when I left almost half of the food on the plate. I went back to my classroom and started to mark a few books. I found I had difficulty in controlling the pen and my writing was becoming so small that it was clearly not acceptable. For some reason I had become unbelievably stressed and there was no explanation. That evening at home I cried because I felt so utterly wretched. The next morning, a Saturday, my wife insisted that I attend the "Walk in Clinic" at Darlington to find some help for my condition.

An Uncertain Future

We have a country cottage in Wales and we were staying there for the weekend. We have decided to come and live here and find a more suitable house which would accommodate my changing condition and help in such ways as to not having to climb the stairs or at least to have stairs that would accommodate a stair lift.

I was sitting on the edge of the bed having just awoken and looking out of the window at the beautiful garden when I clearly saw an outdoor all weather green tennis court nestling in amongst the trees and foliage. We have no court but the range of colour and difference in perspective gave a realistic impression of a court.

At the bottom of the garden partly hidden by a tree is a light green caravan. It is old and in disrepair. However the lighter green imagery merging with the darker garden green gave an outline of a tennis court which could be clearly seen. The silver chrome along the side of the caravan and reflected in the morning sun was clearly the top of the tennis net!

How I wished I could just get up and stroll down to the court and enjoy the pleasure of hitting a few balls. Not in a competitive sense but just to play a few rallies and to experience the real pleasure when the racket swing is natural and hits through the ball the sound of which indicates how correctly the shot has been played.

I was thinking sadly that the time may come soon when I can no longer play. I have injured my elbow and am not sure how serious it is. I tore the rotator cuff playing tennis and it was almost a year before it was fully healed. I also tore my medial ligament in my knee playing squash and it was also a considerable time before I had the confidence to play again. What will I feel if this injury to my elbow equally takes such a long time to mend! Parkinson's is a degenerative condition and I know my movements have recently worsened.

I looked out of the window at the court and began to feel slightly despondent that I may not be able to play much longer. Then I thought well I still have my memories of all those special times which have so enhanced my life and which I can so effortlessly recall.

I was interested to know the extent to which my vision of the court was a kind of hallucination or more simply the result of poor eyesight. Perhaps it was a figment of my imagination because I so wished to play. I called next door and asked my neighbour's son who was on holiday if I could ask a favour of him. I wanted him to take a photograph from the position where I sat looking out through the window. I explained what I had seen and asked him if he also could visualise a tennis court at the bottom of the garden. He was an engineer by profession and he explained in detail how certain objects within my field of vision lent increased perspective to what I viewed. Yes, he too could see the court! Look closely at the photograph what do you see?

A readjustment to a competitive need

There were many changes I needed to accept if I was to cope with my decreased mobility and to be rational about the likelihood of further impairment to my ease of movement. The difficulties are further enhanced by the degree of arthritis in my back and joints. At the time I broke my scapula the doctor had told me that some time in the distant future I would require a shoulder replacement.

Parkinson's restricts some of life's pleasures in that you have to lead a more ordered life. It is important to take the medication at precisely the prescribed time each day. You have to curtail your drinking even beyond the safe limits and have your meals at regular times and be extra careful about your diet. I cannot go out for a run in the countryside or even go for an extended walk. I cannot support my favourite football team, Carlisle United, because of the difficulty in getting to the ground and I definitely could not stand in the terraces, which I prefer because my legs would not support me for that length of time.

I could mention many more restrictions but I emphasize these to clarify that more than ever I need to continue to play tennis and to retain the joys of participation with particular regard to the competitive aspect. My initial thoughts were that this could not be done but the coaches at David Lloyd Centre at Stockton-on-Tees helped me to come to terms with a modified session, which not only improved some of the technical aspects of my game but, more importantly, allowed me to play within a structure which offered a competitive challenge. Coaches, "Jo" Paddy, Tom and Philip all helped me to gain the maximum pleasure of the hour-long session. However it was "Jo" especially, the North East & Cumbria Tennis Development Manager for tennis, employed by the Lawn Tennis Association who helped me to gain a pleasure from tennis again ~~that~~ I had not expected.

People often asked me when I was younger how long I would continue to play before retiring from the game. I often replied probably when I am about 70 years old. Well, I am 70 now and more than ever I need to keep playing and enjoy the thrill of occasionally striking the odd ball perfectly and to continue to experience the adrenal rush of competition.

At the start of each hour-long session the coach and I would rally from the baseline concentrating on stroke technique and ensuring the ball is hit deep to the baseline. After about twenty minutes I needed to have a short rest. Then I would practice volleying from close to the net. The prominent weakness of my game from a very early age was my reluctance to volley. I attempted to guide the ball into court rather than punching it. I can recall so many occasions on big points when a lack of pace on this shot allowed my opponent to hit the ball past me. Uninhibited by the need to win the point I found my volleying improving. It may be that in reverting to a competitive situation the volley would be less secure, but nevertheless it has made me feel more competent and increased my enjoyment on the court. My wife came to see me practising one day and was amazed at how much my volleying had improved.

After a further rest we would progress to linking these skills together. We would rally from the back of the court and when the opportunity presented itself I would advance to the net and attempt to volley the ball for a winner. To practise this association of skills it requires a coach or a very skilful player to feed the ball exactly to the right place.

It would be naive of me to suggest that I could transfer this increased level of skill to a situation more competitively presented but it still gives me immense pleasure to strike the ball well from the base line and to advance forward when tactically appropriate and to finish with a decisive volley. We can all dream that we could do this in a more demanding competitive situation. If it is a form of wish-fulfillment, then so be it! Often when I drove home from leaving the Centre I would recall the number of "winning" shots and be determined to improve on it next time.

Another practice which is more demanding and will of course be dependent upon your level of skill and degree of mobility is to use half of the court and play up to ten points. Standing behind the base line on the forehand court the server begins by bouncing the ball once and playing it into the forehand court. To win the point you need to use the width of the court to your maximum advantage and then perhaps to move up and play a winning volley!

I found this practice particularly demanding. As well as testing my movement and fitness to its very limit the tactical variations and controlled shots using every available space made the challenge particularly realistic with regards to satisfying the competitive need. Of course the coach can vary aspects such as allowing two points for a volleyed winner or in relation to some other shot which has been practised.

The coach, more skilful than myself, would vary the difficulty of placement depending on the existing score. Despite being aware of this it was and is enormous fun and exhilarating when the coach struggles occasionally to return one of your shots.

CHAPTER FIFTEEN

THE JOYS OF VETERAN TENNIS

Ethos and its fulfillment in satisfying the competitive instinct.

◉ ◉ ◉

V ETERAN TENNIS HAS been one of the great joys of my life. The competitive challenge of singles events has always been my particular focus although I have always entered the doubles events where this was possible. My more defensive kind of game and reluctance in seeking opportunities to volley meant that I was always more likely to achieve success in singles events. It particularly helped me to exorcise some of the demons of the past in where in County Hard Court Singles events I had never achieved success. My ambition had always been to be regarded as a satisfactory County player and one who earned his place.

At veteran level over a twenty year span I won singles matches against twelve different counties and also against the Isle of Man. In all I won 21 singles matches in County matches. My tournaments successes are listed in the Appendix. This was in marked contrast to the difficulties I had in stepping up from the Junior ranks where I was my school, city and County singles champion. The restrictions placed upon me in my early exposure to County singles events prevented me from gaining the confidence I needed for further improvement.

I was 46 when Doug. Popper began to initiate the groundwork to enter a Cumbrian veterans team into the newly formed National Veterans' Leagues. His commitment was immense and in addition to recruiting players and organising those early league matches he organised practice sessions for his County players and encouraged them in their commitment to veteran tennis.

We did not win a match for almost two years but we were gradually improving and the strong bond between us began to achieve significant improvement. We started to win matches regularly and at one stage moved up two divisions. The statistics do not reveal the immense pleasure we felt in accepting the challenge and achieving such success.

We had some wonderful times together at places we travelled to to play our matches. Some of our wives came with us and we played matches in popular tourist areas such as Oxford, Cambridge, Winchester, Shropshire and Staffordshire. We played against Warwickshire at the Boat Club where they play their County matches. The grass courts are in excellent condition and with the river running alongside and the castle showing in the distance it is a special experience to be there. Our home matches in the Lake District were played at different venues and the opposition were always appreciative of the welcome we gave them.

Over these years our friendships increased and added a new dimension to our lives. We played the game that we loved among the friends we had become and in places which were of particular interest. Many of these matches were repeated over the years and so we were constantly revisiting teams and individual players who had given us such enjoyable matches in the past. As we moved out of the 45+ group into the next higher age group Frank Underwood from Maryport brought along his team to take his place in the group previously occupied by ourselves.

One of the great successes of veteran tennis is that you are playing players of approximate age. Naturally our skill level and fitness declines with age but in playing players of a similar age it helps to rebalance the equation and to provide a continuing competitive challenge. This could stretch from 45+ to beyond 80+ Despite the eagerly awaited challenge we become more philosophical as we age and winning and losing become less intense and provide a further opportunity for pleasure.

In addition to playing at Wimbledon each year and in club and County matches, I also played in three tournaments each year. I played at Doncaster in the Yorkshire Open and won the Singles event twice. However on both these occasions the Yorkshire veteran team had to rearrange the date of their match when the original date was altered because of the death of the Princess Diana. The unbeaten Yorkshire veteran team were representing England in the European Tournament. Of the four players in this team and who played regularly in the Doncaster Tournament I had never beaten apart from a doubles specialist who I had beaten twice in a singles event. Paul Ranson, the captain of the team and who also reached the final of the World Father and Son event and lost narrowly in the final to Newcome and Son, has beaten me on 6 occasions and the most success I have had was in the last time I played him when I was able to salvage a set! In my first appearance at Doncaster I reached the final of both the mens and mixed doubles but beaten in both events.

In the Huddersfield Tournament I won the singles event on two occasions and one of them by the misfortune of a player who couldn't play in the semi final because he had reached the final of a doubles event in the prestigious Eastbourne tournament which was being played on the same day. He had twice beaten me in the past. However, it was in this tournament that along with my friend Youseff Khan we won our first doubles title in over twenty years and retained the title the following year. Both matches were closely fought. In the first we led 4-3 in the third and final set when their net player at 30-40 down appeared to have made a successful anticipation of a forehand return from Youseff hit wide to the forehand court and at an inviting height but the opponent lost the point when he volleyed it just long. At match point Youseff served wide to the forehand court and the weak return gave an opportunity to smash which Youseff appeared to accept. However at the last moment he checked his racket momentum and played a drop shot. It was an unexpected shot and the ball bounced twice before the opponent realised what had happened. Youseff, normally calm and undemonstrative, punched the air in delight; it was a special moment for both of us.

My favourite tournament other than Wimbledon was at Ilkley. There are 21 well maintained grass courts set in an idyllic surrounding and the tournament is a week long. In the large field leading to the cars field there is also room to pitch your tent. For many years a number of players and their coach would come from Holland to enjoy their tennis and have a holiday. One year I was drawn against the clubs coach and won after a particularly long struggle. Later that day I passed several young players who had watched the game and who congratulated me on winning. What a kindness, I thought.

On four occasions I reached the men's singles final in the 45+ and 55+ and twice in the 60+ event. On each occasion I was well beaten, with perhaps the last the exception. It was against Trevor Nuthall who had previously beaten me in one of the finals and several times in rounds leading to the final. I took the second set off him by a more attacking game but he was playing well below his normal form. He lost the set rather than I won it. We even discussed this at the end of the second set! Perhaps I had resigned myself too easily to always losing to him.

One always felt part of a special scene at Ilkley. There were the satellite matches you could watch where some of the best up and coming players struggled for recognition in a very competitive environment. In the evenings you could see the earnest endeavor of the veteran matches and, at times, the light hearted nature of some of the local tennis enthusiasts playing in some of the handicap events. Then there were the evening singles matches which often produced a very high standard of play; Ilkley catered for all the skilful and enthusiastic players and encouraged those who merely wanted to watch and to be part of an enjoyable occasion. Whenever I walked into Ilkley and saw the courts full of enthusiastic players looked up at the balcony restaurant where players would often watch the tennis from and observe players coming to and fro from the Referee's desk either going out to play or confirming a result, I felt part of a very special occasion and knew I was going to enjoy the remainder of the day.

A FINAL THOUGHT . . .

◉ ◉ ◉

S PORT, A MICROCOSM of human life, offers us the opportunity to learn from our mistakes. Those moments in our own game which I refer to as a psychological hurdle should be faced head on and eliminated by using every available source to assist you in overcoming this problem. After coming to terms with the mechanics of the shot we need to practice it and again and again until our confidence returns and we relish the opportunity to demonstrate our new found skill.

In my writings the most significant change I have outlined has been the enhanced opportunity to play and the easy access to profit from the coach's knowledge. The coach can notice things in your game which you have not seen or are unaware that it is happening. A correction accompanied by concentrated practice will soon display a marked improvement in your game.

Players are often characterised by being known as a defensive player or an attacking player. My game was essentially based on my fitness and retrieving skills and brought me some success in club and tournament matches. However when one meets a more accomplished opponent you find that they, too, can maintain a long rally and allied to their defensive skills their greater repertoire and range of skill overcomes you. This does not mean hitting the cover off the ball or an outright winner each time but patiently and strategically building up a momentum in the rally whereby a weaker return can be exploited by the use of your new found attacking shots.

I have empathised how tennis can satisfy our need for the competitive instinct to be challenged and adjustments made in our expectations of success because of factors such as age, injuries and health related matters.

In some sports we seem to have moved from an Age of Innocence to an Age of Deceit. Tennis still retains its integrity and opportunity for the display of life enhancing experiences. We need to maintain its unique quality.

About The Authors

❧ ❧ ❧

Howard Nixon from an early age was interested in the academic enquiries relating theory to sporting performance. An honours Diploma from Loughborough College and Master of Science and Master of Arts degrees from Massachusetts and Leeds Universities enabled him to pursue his interests and, as a Senior Lecturer in Physical Education, he lectured in Colleges of Education on the degree courses.

He was the Cumberland County Junior tennis champion and played for them in Inter County Week. As a veteran player he won four singles titles in L.T.A. Open veteran tournaments and played at Wimbledon and Bournemouth in the National Veteran Tournaments. Despite his modest achievements, he recalls the excitement and pleasure of club and tournament play. His recollections reveal his innermost thoughts about the challenges and rewards of competitive play. Now suffering from Parkinson's disease he continues to play twice weekly and maintain his love and enthusiasm for the game.

Jo Cunliffe is a former England and Great Britain Junior international player. Following her junior career, she decided to concentrate on coaching tennis. Now the L.T.A. Development Manager for the North East and Cumbria she was recently awarded the prestigious "colleague of the year award" for her significant contribution to tennis. She has coached Howard during recent years and has become a close friend.

Tournament Results — Howard Nixon

Junior Tournaments

Austin Friars School	Singles Winner
Carlisle Municipal U16 Tournament	Singles Winner
Carlisle Municipal U18 Tournament	Singles Winner (2 years running)
Cumberland Tournament U18	Singles Finalist
Cumberland Tournament U18	Singles Winner
Cumberland Tournament Mens	Singles Handicap Winner (Senior Event)
Nithsdale Tournament	Mens Singles Handicap Winner (Senior Event)
Cumberland Open U21	Mens Doubles
Cumberland Open U18	Mixed Doubles Finalist

Senior Tournaments

Cottingham LT Club Hull	Mens Singles Winner x2, Finalist x1
English Martyrs LT Club Manchester	Mens Singles Winner x4
New Blackwell Club, Darlington	Mens Singles Winner, Finalist x2
Rhos on Sea LTC	Mens Singles Winner, Mens Singles Handicap Winner
Keswick Open	Mens Doubles Winner Mens Doubles Handicap Finalist
Cottingham LTC	Mens Doubles Winner
New Allotment	Mens Doubles Finalist x4
Keswick Open	Mixed Doubles Finalist
New Blackwell Club	Mixed Doubles Winner
Rhos on Sea LTC	Mixed Doubles Finalist

Veteran Events

Yorkshire Open O55	Mens Singles Winner x2, Finalist x2
Cumbria Veterans O55	Mens Singles Winner x2, Finalist x1
Huddersfield O55 and O60	Mens Singles Winner x2, Finalist x2
North-East Regional T.C. Darlington	Mens Singles Winner Mens Doubles Winner
Yorkshire Open O45	Mens Doubles Finalist Mixed Doubles Finalist
Huddersfield Open	Mens Doubles Winner x2

Yorkshire Open	Mixed Doubles Finalist
Rhos on Sea LTC	Mixed Doubles Finalist
Ilkley Tournament	Mens Singles Finalist +45
	Mens Singles Finalist +55 x2
	Mens Singles Finalist +60

Lightning Source UK Ltd.
Milton Keynes UK
UKOW050818150612

194457UK00001B/9/P